THE RETURN OF THE STATE

THE RETURN OF THE STATE

AND WHY IT IS ESSENTIAL FOR OUR HEALTH,
WEALTH AND HAPPINESS

GRAEME GARRARD

YALE UNIVERSITY PRESS
NEW HAVEN AND LONDON

For information about this and other Yale University Press publications, please contact:
U.S. Office: sales.press@yale.edu   yalebooks.com
Europe Office: sales@yaleup.co.uk   yalebooks.co.uk

Set in Adobe Garamond Regular by IDSUK (DataConnection) Ltd
Printed in Great Britain by TJ Books, Padstow, Cornwall

Library of Congress Control Number: 2022931862

ISBN 978-0-300-25675-8

A catalogue record for this book is available from the British Library.

10 9 8 7 6 5 4 3 2 1

To

David Hanley and James Bernard Murphy

CONTENTS

CONTENTS

ACKNOWLEDGEMENTS

In writing this book I have incurred debts of kindness and support that I am pleased to acknowledge here.

Foremost among these debts are to David Hanley and James Murphy, who have been constant friends and intellectual companions for many years. This book is dedicated to them with my heartfelt gratitude, although this does not imply their agreement with its contents.

This project was conceived and developed in close consultation with my agent Jaime Marshall. I am grateful to him for guiding me so deftly through this process and giving me the benefit of his considerable knowledge and wisdom.

I owe the London team at Yale University Press, Joanna Godfrey, Felicity Maunder, Lucy Buchan, Heather Nathan, Charlotte Chapman, and all of their colleagues who contributed to the production of this book, my appreciation for their patience and professionalism in bringing it to press. I am especially thankful for Joanna Godfrey's belief in the project and her encouragement throughout.

I am grateful to Yale University Press's anonymous reviewers of this book's manuscript for their thoughtful and constructive suggestions for improvement.

Andrew Dowling and his family – Nkiru, Maya and Erin – have provided me with many hours of welcome distraction from the innumerable vexations and absurdities of professional academic life, for which I am grateful.

I owe my appreciation in one way or another to many other people, amongst whom are Craig Patterson, David Boucher, Steve Marsh, Carole Pateman, Ulrich Schöllwock, Sean Loughlin, Nick Parsons, Christopher Miles, Peter Sedgwick, my parents, and my aunt and late uncle.

INTRODUCTION

In mid-Victorian Britain, in the bleak world of Charles Dickens before the welfare state existed, access to healthcare was almost entirely a matter of social class. The tiny upper class and most of the middle class (then very small) paid for their medical treatment out of their own pockets. The doctor's basic fee of sixpence plus the cost of the medicines he prescribed were beyond the means of the vast majority of people. A home visit by a private doctor enabled the well off to avoid going to a hospital, which was then widely seen as a thoroughly unhealthy place.

For the rest there was a system of voluntary hospitals supported by charities and staffed by volunteers, and publicly funded (and underfunded) workhouse infirmaries. The lucky few were admitted as patients to voluntary hospitals, which accounted for about a third of all hospital beds in England by the early twentieth century. Sometimes individuals were required to make some financial contribution to their care if it was judged that they could afford it, although most were charged nothing. Membership in a community-owned mutual aid fund, medical club or work-related insurance scheme enabled some working men to pay small regular premiums to cover the cost of healthcare should it be needed, particularly for medicines, although their family members were not usually covered.

For the destitute poor there was the dreaded workhouse, which Ebenezer Scrooge cruelly commended for 'their useful course'. These grim institutions, so powerfully evoked by Dickens in his novel *Oliver Twist*, were the last resort of those who could find no other work. Workhouse inmates laboured in return for a meagre subsistence. If they became ill, as they often did in such conditions, they were kept in the crowded, unsanitary and badly ventilated infirmary where they received the most rudimentary care from overworked and often demoralised (and not infrequently drunk) doctors.

Imagine what the world would be like today in a global pandemic under such a Malthusian system, even if a vaccine was available. Your health would depend on the whims of charity, your ability to pay private corporations or your place in a hierarchical client–patron network. Think more generally of a world of private, for-profit monopolies demanding payment for primary and secondary education, healthcare, access to roads and ports, police protection, the running of prisons and the military.

INTRODUCTION

The revolution in publicly funded health and welfare that occurred in the West between 1850 and 1950 reflected a growing belief in the fundamental unfairness of such an arbitrary system, where ability to pay played a dominant part in people's lives. Most wealthier states now provide all of their citizens with access to some form of publicly funded healthcare as a basic right, the US being a notable exception. But for several centuries after the emergence of states in the early-modern period, the health and welfare of the general population was considered no part of their purpose or responsibility. Churches and charities provided virtually all such care for the vast majority who could not afford it themselves. Today, universal, publicly funded healthcare is one of the greatest achievements of the state in those parts of the world that are wealthy enough to afford it and decent enough to provide it.

This system is not now under threat of collapse or reverting to what preceded it. But it is on the defensive and has been for some time now. It is beleaguered and demeaned, subject to constant outsourcing, privatisation, marketisation and austerity measures by a political ideology that seeks to 'roll back the frontiers of the state'. This deliberate political project has been underway for a generation now and has done massive cumulative damage to many of the most vulnerable while profiting many of the most well off. Political and economic elites have their own resources to pay for such services privately, so they have little 'skin in the game' of this welfare system, as they don't suffer the direct consequences of underfunding it.

Things are very much worse for people in many poorer parts of the world, like Somalia, where the state barely exists. After 1991 it was not only a land without peace but it lacked the basic public goods that many states now provide to their citizens, such as education, healthcare, a well-maintained transportation and communications infrastructure and a regular system of laws. The plight of Somalia at the time (and to some degree since) is a nightmare vision of life without any functioning state. While it is an extreme example, since states rarely collapse completely, it serves to remind us of what we take for granted about the state.

Almost four centuries ago the English state failed, creating a political vacuum in which a civil war caused the deaths of tens of thousands (proportionately, the equivalent today of almost two million people). This led the English philosopher Thomas Hobbes to write one of the first and most influential defences of the state, which he called *Leviathan* (1651) after the biblical sea-monster. He only narrowly escaped with his life when he changed sides – twice – in that conflict. In his eyes, the only realistic alternative to a strong state was anarchy, literally 'no rule', a condition in which no one is safe, he thought. He saw a strong state as the *only* way to keep the peace, without which life would be, in his famous phrase, 'solitary, poor, nasty, brutish and short'.

But the modern state now looks increasingly like a beached whale rather than the mighty leviathan state of Hobbes. Today it is gripped by a new kind of crisis. The state is being increasingly challenged by the rise of new powers that did not exist in the seventeenth century. These are subverting its capacity to protect citizens and act for the public good. While states are retreating from active involvement in the market through widespread privatisations, outsourcing and deregulation, corporations are rapidly expanding their wealth and power. Today half of the hundred largest economies in the world are private corporations.[1] Apple, Amazon, Microsoft and Alphabet/Google are each worth more than the GDP of 168 nations. If the state continues to be whittled away from within and eclipsed by these mega-corporations from without, the lives and well-being of most of us will be increasingly subject to unaccountable corporate powers driven exclusively by their own interests. In Hobbes's time, a weak or failed state meant anarchy and civil war; in our time, it means potentially despotic rule by private, profit-seeking powers that serve the interests of the few, leaving the many at their mercy. In most countries the state now provides a whole range of public goods beyond just physical security (Hobbes's paramount concern), such as health, education, welfare and culture. But caught between the rise of regional governments, sub-state movements and powerful globalising forces, the state as we have known it since World War Two has been gradually ground down, sold off, delegitimated and increasingly marginalised.

I am not predicting that the state will completely collapse or 'wither away' under capitalism, as Friedrich Engels imagined it would under communism, although that may be a realistic possibility in some rare cases. The state is not dying. Indeed, it has increased its capacity in some areas, such as the surveillance of its own citizens, owing to advances in technology. And its spending sometimes increases as a percentage of GDP, as it did during the 2008 financial crisis and, more recently, during the Coronavirus pandemic. Most government spending in most developed countries is on health, welfare and pensions, although these services have all been subject to incessant long-term privatisation, austerity regimes and outsourcing. Even so, states in the neoliberal West and in large parts of the world that are under its economic hegemony have retreated significantly from direct involvement in markets, which they prefer to leave more or less alone except when they fail. Then they come running with money to bail out supposedly too-big-to-fail banks and businesses whose collapse threatens to bring the whole house down. States are losing their capacity to act effectively in a global economy increasingly led and dominated by multinational corporations whose sole motivation is profit.

These changes to the state since, roughly, the late 1970s were neither accidental nor inevitable. They are primarily the result of deliberate policies by those who subscribe to the ideology of neoliberalism, according to which unimpeded capitalist markets are the fairest, most efficient and most cost-effective way to run an economy and promote general well-being. It became the dominant ideology and principal political project of many countries, epitomised by British prime minister Margaret Thatcher but by no means confined to the political right. It led to policies such as deregulation of the economy (particularly financial markets), privatisation of public utilities, the outsourcing of government functions to the private sector, reductions to impediments to the free movement of people, goods and capital, and the elimination of price controls.

The state's diminishing capacity to act for the public good is especially dangerous in the absence of any other agency in the world realistically capable of countering the growing power of rival entities, such as multinational corporations, international organisations, drug cartels, terrorist networks, organised crime and technology-driven social media companies, that will always put their own interests first. For people and organisations who are dependent on it, as almost all of us now are, the retreat of the state poses a very real danger, as the agencies that replace it are likely to be unwilling or unable to protect and support the lives of ordinary people to the extent that they have been used to for the last seventy-five years in the West. Now, only the state has the power and potential to protect and promote public goods, individual rights and general welfare from unelected non-state powers that pursue their own private agendas, unanswerable to the majority and increasingly free from external scrutiny and control. If the state is weakened sufficiently, we will face a bleak future that looks more like the nineteenth than the twentieth century, where the lives of most people are governed by capricious local oligarchs and access to vital goods and resources is directly dependent on an individual's status, wealth and power.

Sceptics on both the left and the right correctly point out that the state and the market have often colluded against the general interest, more mutually supportive than antagonistic. The Scottish economist Adam Smith noticed this tendency almost 250 years ago when he observed with concern that 'the English legislature has been peculiarly attentive to the interest of commerce and manufactures', even when this had been harmful to the public good. What was to Smith in the eighteenth century a worrisome cosiness between business and the state was to Marx and Engels in the nineteenth century the complete subordination of the state to capitalism. 'The executive of the modern State', they wrote in 1848, 'is but a committee for managing the common affairs of the whole bourgeoisie'.[2] And in the twentieth century the anarcho-syndicalist Noam Chomsky echoed Marx's views in his own influential assaults on the 'State–Corporate Nexus'.

This outlook is by no means confined to the left. Recent 'civil society' conservatives like Phillip Blond in the UK and Patrick Deneen in the US share this idea of the state and the market as co-conspirators against the commonweal. Blond rejects both the modern welfare state for fostering authoritarian gigantism and the free market for promoting selfish individualism. His alternative is the 'Big Society', a realm between state and market rich with freely associating groups such as churches, charities, schools, pubs, clubs and small local businesses that support and strengthen social bonds without encouraging the growth of giant market monopolies and a leviathan state. Deneen portrays contemporary states and markets as aspects of a single liberal pathology that has dissolved traditional communitarian attachments that are essential to any healthy form of collective life. For state-sceptics on the left and the right, freedom can only be found beyond the market and the state in 'civil society', the so-called 'third sector' of free, independent associations.

But civil society has been too thoroughly penetrated and colonised by market forces to offer any kind of realistic alternative now. Its 'little platoons' are nowhere near strong or numerous enough to resist the pervasive power and influence of global markets and consumer culture in our lives, which have been greatly magnified by technology. It is a fantasy to think that there is, or could be, a 'Big Society' to which we can turn to escape the overbearing power of the Big Market. The only plausible check on big business today is the Big State. This is our only realistic option now and for the foreseeable future for challenging the growing power and influence of multi-national corporations.

A Big State, but not the Biggest State. A state that is too big may be weakened by overextension, dissipating its power and resources by trying to do too much. No state has infinite resources and limitless knowledge. All states must have priorities and allocate resources according to them. Some hard choices are unavoidable. There is an optimal point beyond which state power diminishes as its size increases, an ideal spot where it is strong enough to control runaway market forces without itself becoming oppressive or ineffective. In the West today, we have fallen short of this point and we have not found the best balance between private profit and broader social goods. This is partly because of the dominance of an ideology that naively assumes that markets are almost always the best way to provide such goods. But it isn't just the consequence of ideology warping perceptions of how capitalism really works. Self-interest has also played a big part in the popularity of these policies among political and economic elites, who are usually their principal beneficiaries.

It would be foolish to deny that state power entails very significant risks. But so does market power. And while strong states are dangerous, so are weak states, as Hobbes knew well. There is no risk-free option. Debates about the state should therefore be about the degree and nature of the risks that each poses. And this requires an understanding of the risks that markets pose, which are considerable and growing, although too often underestimated, particularly in the West.

We are now in an age of monopoly and oligopoly capitalism. There is no realistic alternative to this in which many small and medium-sized firms compete in a free market that is efficient, fair and responsible, except in economics textbooks and ideological tracts, neither of which are reliable guides to the real world. A small number of mega-corporations now dominate the global economy and account for a growing share of its wealth and power. These are either private, as in the West, or public, as they often are in the Far East and parts of the Global South. Those are now our options.

The trend towards greater private power at the expense of public power is not uniform across the world. In many developing countries the balance still favours the state. It is even fair to speak of a resurgence of state capitalism in some regions, where the state acts as the dominant economic power and can act for the public good, even if it doesn't always do so.[3] The leader of this approach is China, where only three of its forty-two biggest companies are privately owned and state enterprises account for a third of all capital spending, compared to just 5 per cent in most developed economies.[4] In many countries outside the West today China's statist approach to its economy is an increasingly popular alternative to the neoliberal orthodoxy favoured by elites in most developed countries and by the international financial agencies such as the International Monetary Fund (IMF) and the World Bank that they dominate. This new statist trend began even before the crisis of 2008, when it accelerated rapidly. In the four years prior to this, 117 state-owned firms in Brazil, Russia, India and China were included in the Forbes Global 2000 list of the world's largest companies, while 239 privately owned Western companies were knocked off it.[5] State-owned companies today control 75 per cent of the world's oil reserves.[6] Even within the West there has been a recent shift (albeit probably temporary) towards more direct state involvement in economic life in response to the 2008 financial crisis and the Covid-19 pandemic, although there has not yet been any general movement to renationalise parts of the economy.

Taking a major step in the direction of state capitalism and more active, direct government involvement in economic life does not necessarily require political authoritarianism of the kind practised in China today, despite the claims of some of its opponents. It is neither unrealistic nor unprecedented for popular governments to assert the public interest this way, particularly at a time when trust in free market capitalism around the world is declining, particularly among the young.[7] It is only since the neoliberal wave of privatisations, deregulation and outsourcing that began in the 1970s that the state has increasingly removed itself from the business of business, except when it has jumped in temporarily to bail corporations out of their own folly.

It is natural to be ambivalent about the state because it is reasonable to fear that an entity powerful enough to do so much good is also powerful enough to do a great deal of bad. Certainly the modern state is not an easy thing to love, with its lumbering bureaucracy, arbitrary borders and reputation for violence. That's why it has never lacked enemies. The state has been attacked from every angle, left, right and centre, and in every age since it first emerged in its modern form four centuries ago. Popular attitudes to the state tend to be less rigid than those of ideologues and are more influenced by changing circumstances. Events since early 2020 have reminded us of some of the good and the bad that it can do. While the state is an abstraction, it is a very concrete and immediate reality in our daily lives, although it often takes a crisis to remind us of this. The Covid pandemic has shown that, at its best, the state can and does play a highly positive, sometimes even lifesaving, role in the lives of many people today. But it has also provoked a backlash against what some perceive as excessive control that threatens civil liberties, leading to demonstrations and protests in many parts of the world.

The balance between state power and market power is constantly shifting. We have been living in an era when the balance tilted towards business to a dangerous degree. But very recently it has shifted back somewhat towards the state because of the financial crisis of 2008 and the Covid-19 virus, the worst pandemic since the 1918 Spanish flu. Although many failures and mistakes have been made in response to this global crisis, and many lives lost as a result, vaccines were developed and administered in much of the world in record time, public health services were mobilised and adapted to treat the afflicted on a global scale, and governments have dispensed vast amounts of money to support businesses forced to close and workers facing possible ruin by prolonged and repeated lockdowns and restrictions.

The time has come to restore the balance between states and markets by reasserting greater state control over and involvement in the market to promote the public interest, checking the burgeoning power of private corporations and ensuring greater accountability over the powers that dominate our lives. This means bringing the neoliberal experiment of the last fifty years to a complete end, a process that may already have begun. It also means democratisation of the economy by using the power of the state to make the economy serve the public good rather than the other way round. And it means reversing the incessant privatisation and outsourcing of the welfare mission of the state that ensures the greatest possible access to the full range of public goods that all citizens need to lead fulfilling lives.

The state is the dominant form of organised public power in the world today. That hasn't always been the case. Before the rise of the state in early modernity, the two 'estates' of the church and the aristocracy were predominant. They have now been replaced in that position by the state and the market. It is likely that these will one day be succeeded by new forms of power. But until that happens they are the only two games in town. This book makes the case for a Public Interest State as the best path and the lesser risk. Only states have the potential to ensure there is common provision for those who cannot afford many of the basic ingredients of a good life. The state can be a force for good in a way that profit-maximising corporations never can. The twenty-first-century post-neoliberal world will require a bold return of the state to its proper role as the principal champion of the public good and general welfare.

1

BUILDING A
PEOPLE'S STATE

The state is an enigma. We cannot see it or touch it directly, though we can see and feel its effects, sometimes violently (such as in wars and law enforcement). It is an abstraction, yet it is arguably the most powerful human force on earth today. We all live in states, which are now the main unit of political organisation in the world, and almost the entire planet today is covered by them, yet for most of human history states did not exist. They are a relatively recent invention that might one day cease to exist or become just one power among many, and perhaps not the greatest or most important of them.

The earliest states were small and limited to providing some measure of peace and security for their citizens in a very dangerous world with fairly primitive technology compared to today. They were ruled by small, unelected elites who were unaccountable to those they governed. Most states today are

16

democracies, at least formally, and are expected by their members to provide for their general well-being with free (or publicly subsidised) healthcare, education and welfare. That is mainly why states now are so much larger, richer and stronger than their earliest predecessors.

States do not exist in isolation. They have evolved and adapted constantly in response to the challenges they face, both internally and externally. At first, the power and sovereignty of states were challenged mainly by established religious institutions. Now, their principal rivals are large multinational corporations. The state today has been fundamentally shaped by the existence of this enormous and growing form of private power, which barely existed when the first states were created. Much of the history of the state since the emergence of industrial capitalism in the early nineteenth century has been a struggle between public power, embodied in the state, and private power, in the form of large international corporations. This battle has gone on at many levels, from abstract ideas to the everyday lived experience of ordinary people trying to survive and prosper in a world now dominated by states and corporations.

Inventing the State

Politics has always existed in human history. When the ancient Greek philosopher Aristotle said that 'man is a political animal' he meant that humans naturally form political communities of some kind. It is part of what makes us human. But for most of the life of our species such communities were not states, which is a specific, modern way of conceiving of politics. Until the sixteenth century, non-state forms of governance were the norm, such as tribes, fiefdoms and principalities, although these shared some characteristics with the state as we know it today. In the West now we tend to assume politics and states naturally go together because politics has been intrinsic to the state for several centuries. States first emerged from the fragmentation and chaos of the Middle Ages, mainly to provide a stable structure powerful enough to maintain internal peace and order. In the twentieth century, the purpose of states massively expanded beyond just keeping the peace to include the health and welfare of its members, and its power and cost have expanded proportionately.

Prior to the modern age, government was personal. In the ancient world there was no 'state' understood in abstraction from the people. 'Where we could say "the state"', Martin van Creveld has said of the ancient Greeks and Romans, 'they would write "the public" or "the people".'[1] In feudal Europe, relations of power were based on personal bonds between peasants, lords and kings similar to the members of an extended family, which is why oaths of loyalty were made to specific people rather than to general concepts like the nation, the state or the constitution.

It was not until the sixteenth century that political communities began to be formed into states. The first use of the word 'state' dates from this time, unlike the much older term 'government'.[2] A state was understood to have a specific population, more or less fixed territory and was legally supreme inside its boundaries with a monopoly on the legitimate use of force within it. But what really distinguishes it from non-state forms of government is its abstract and impersonal character.

The territory of a state is not conceived as its ruler's own personal property, as it had been in earlier ages. In modernity, the person of the ruler and his or her 'state' became separated from each other. Previously, when a ruler died the polity they ruled often collapsed or was carved up or seized by others, which is why transitions between rulers were often so messy and violent, like the treacherous world of *Game of Thrones*. By contrast, the modern state survives the death of its ruler and officeholders because its power transcends them. It isn't personal. Servants of the state occupy offices within it; they do not own them and do not wield its power personally either, even if in practice they often act as if they do. A state is a continuous public power with a life of its own, 'above both ruler and ruled which provides order and continuity to the polity'.[3] When the ruler of a state dies their office continues and so does allegiance to the state by its subjects, in theory and usually in practice.

Many writers at this time began to develop new theories to explain and justify the state as a distinctive form of political authority. The most famous and influential of these, by far, is the English philosopher Thomas Hobbes, 'the man who really invented the state'.[4] His book *Leviathan* sets out a fully developed conception of the state as an 'artificial man' that exists as an abstract entity separate from the ruler and his subjects. Writing during the English Civil War (1642–51), he was concerned above all to legitimise a powerful state whose overriding purpose was to provide for the security of those within it. As the philosopher Bernard Williams has put it, the first political question is how to secure 'order, protection, safety, trust and the conditions of cooperation', as these are preconditions for other goods.[5] For Hobbes, the state must above all keep its members physically safe, which European states in the seventeenth century had often disastrously failed to do. Hobbes claimed that the greatest evil that can befall us is the constant fear of violent death that stalks us at every turn outside of the state, where life is a war of all against all. Governments must be judged solely by their 'Aptitude to produce the Peace and Security of the people'.

Hobbes feared that dispersing power within a political community always risked civil war and chaos, particularly in an age when groups were opposed by differences rooted in strong religious convictions. He had personally witnessed this when he lived in France during the devastating Thirty Years War in Europe that led to eight million deaths (military and civilian), the equivalent of eighty million people as a proportion of Europe's total population today. Not only were religious differences fuelling civil conflicts and destabilising governments throughout Europe but technological advances in gunpowder, artillery, small arms design and manufacture, and ballistics were making warfare increasingly deadly.

But the theoretically absolute power of these early modern states was not matched by their actual power, which was practically limited by constraints like a weak infrastructure of roads and bridges, poor communication, and relatively slow and primitive forms of transportation such as horses and sailing ships. It would take several centuries for the real power of the state to catch up with absolute theories of state power like that of Hobbes. The king's sovereignty might have been theoretically limitless but his actual capacity to reach the four corners of his realm was conditioned by natural limits which have since been overcome by technology to a degree unimaginable in the age of the Stuart kings.

The French historian Michel Foucault has argued that it was often the practical weakness of these early states that caused them to make such a grand public spectacle of their power when they could, as in the unfortunate case of Robert-François Damiens. In his book *Discipline and Punish* (1975), Foucault describes the gory and prolonged public torture and execution of this wretched young man for the crime of attempting to assassinate King Louis XV, the personification of the French state, in 1757. He stresses the link between the extremity of the state's power exerted so visibly against this single, defenceless transgressor and the practical limitations and relative poverty of the state compared to the much greater, if more subtle, power of later states. Paradoxically, the almost limitless power of the French state at the time to subdue a single subject was, for Foucault, an expression of the very real limits of its power to control its population in general. Only later, with advances in science and technology, did the capacity of states to monitor and control their populations expand so much that it made totalitarianism possible. We have gone from states that are absolute in theory but very limited in practice to states that are limited in theory but extremely powerful in practice.

The Classical State

It was concern over the potential power of the state that convinced some thinkers and statesmen to try to design and justify political systems that would limit it. Foremost among them is the English philosopher John Locke, who argued in the seventeenth century that states are only legitimate when they protect their members' natural rights to life, liberty and property. Whereas Hobbes had argued that any limits on the power of the state would destroy it, leading to chaos, Locke believed that an overbearing state that trampled on individual rights would be worse than no state. For Hobbes there is nothing worse than no state.

It is little wonder that Locke had such a huge influence on the founding fathers of the United States, who violently opposed just such an overbearing state (as they saw it) in the person of King George III. They successfully rebelled against him in defence of their rights and then designed their own Lockean political system of checks and balances with a written constitution to constrain sovereign power. This was the beginning of the classical liberal idea of a limited, constitutional state that eventually became dominant in the English-speaking world in the nineteenth century. Liberal democracy is now the most common form of democratic state, although it is unlikely to remain so.

Opponents of this liberal view of the state on the right at the time objected that it was too weak to maintain social and political order and was dangerously indifferent to the moral character of the people. Many also objected to the secularisation of the state, believing in the inseparability of throne and altar. They were certain that Locke's minimal state would not, and should not, last. By the nineteenth century some of these paternalistic conservative opponents of the classical liberal state also criticised it on humanitarian grounds for ignoring the plight of the poor, particularly those who worked like slaves in factories or were left destitute and abandoned in the rapidly swelling cities of early industrial capitalism. The Edwardian politician Hugh Cecil reminded his fellow Conservatives of this when he wrote not long before World War One:

That authority should relieve suffering; that it should control and regulate trade; that it should restrain luxury; that it should suppress vice; that it should maintain religious truth – these were principles which appealed to our forefathers as reasonable and especially to those among them who were Tories. And in the nineteenth century, when Liberalism enforced to the utmost the principle of personal liberty, it was among Conservatives that the authority and control of the State was defended and in some instances enlarged and strengthened.[6]

Classical liberals and traditional conservatives at the time disagreed fundamentally on the purpose of the state, with the former limiting it to the role of 'policeman that guards to every man his own' by protecting life, liberty and property, while the latter believed that it should also provide for the physical and moral health of the people, as they saw it. By the middle of the twentieth century these positions would be completely reversed, with 'conservatives', as classical liberals now call themselves, arguing for a limited state, and contemporary 'liberals' usually defending greater state power.

To the left of the classical liberals in the nineteenth century, anarchists and Marxists saw the state in all of its forms as inherently oppressive and called for its eventual abolition in favour of a spontaneously self-regulating communist society. Although they disagreed passionately on how best to bring

this about, like Hobbes they saw the state as essentially negative, a purely coercive apparatus at the disposal of the ruling
class to compel the people to obey. The German sociologist
Max Weber had defined the state as 'the only human community which lays claim to the monopoly on the legitimate use
of force' in the form of police and armies which can be
deployed internally against their own citizens and externally
against other states and their populations. For Marx, the state
is never anything more than an extension of the power of the
ruling class. The brutal destruction of the revolutionary
socialist Paris Commune by the French military in 1871 was
seen by Marx as confirmation of his view that the state is just
a blunt instrument used by the rich and powerful to beat
down the unruly masses.

Unlike traditional conservative critics of the classical liberal
state at the time, who wanted it to curb the excesses of industrial capitalism, Marx and the anarchists rejected this on the
grounds that, in bourgeois societies, states always and necessarily serve the interests of the wealthy. However, some socialists like the German writer and political activist Ferdinand
Lassalle, much abused verbally by Marx, agreed with conservatives like Otto von Bismarck that the state was not simply the
capitalists' handmaiden and could, in the right hands, act
with some independence to improve the well-being of workers.
Today, the negative Marxist view of the state is ironically most
commonly found among right-wing libertarians.

Marx's emphasis on coercive force as the essence of the state – of *all* states – is exaggerated, since it is obvious that they do a great deal more than just bludgeon people over the head, even if they sometimes do that, and worse. Unlike Lassalle, he completely failed to predict the advent of the welfare state and labour laws that would greatly improve the condition of working people within capitalist societies. But Marx is certainly right that physical power and a 'State–Corporate Nexus' are essential features of all modern states. The 1926 General Strike and the miners' strike in Britain in 1984–5, both of which were forcefully suppressed, show the brutal reality of state power when directed against elements of the working class who challenge it.

Modern states not only maintain large standing armies and navies but, beginning with Napoleon, have imposed mass conscription on their citizens to fight major wars, which had become increasingly lethal because of huge technological advances since the second half of the nineteenth century. The American Civil War is a good example of how the combination of modern military technology and mass conscription can turn the state into a deadly killing machine, the coldest of all cold monsters, as the philosopher Friedrich Nietzsche branded it. A lucrative 'military–industrial complex' has grown up between the state and private corporations in many countries to develop and manufacture new weapons in a proliferating arms race between the world's major powers that continues to this day.

While the United States is perhaps the best contemporary example of this collusion between the state and the defence industry, it existed in the German empire until its defeat in World War One and still exists today in Britain, France, Russia and China. For example, in 2019 defence contract spending by the US government was over \$400 billion, much of it going to a relatively small number of corporations. A well-established revolving door leads straight from the Pentagon to these companies that hire a steady stream of retired military personnel to advise them on the requirements of warfare and, more importantly, to lobby governments on their behalf.[7] A similar pattern exists in Britain, where a disturbing number of senior Ministry of Defence civil servants, military staff and government ministers end up employed by arms manufacturers, each of which receive millions of pounds in government contracts every year. Although an Advisory Committee on Business Appointments (ACOBA) is meant to act as a watchdog on this process, it has advisory powers only and is not very effective in stopping the military–industrial revolving door from spinning. And you will struggle to distinguish between the senior command of the Russian military and the boardrooms of the leading Russian defence contractors. The same is true of China.

This is not a uniquely military problem. Governments all over the world are full of revolving doors connecting the senior echelons of the state (civil servants and politicians) with corporate boardrooms. The staff of regulatory agencies are particularly prone to switch from gamekeepers to poachers. That is why French law requires public officials to wait for three years before they can work in the private sector after leaving government service, although this is exceptional and still doesn't completely solve the problem.[8] This process occasionally works in the opposite direction as well; governments sometimes hire people from private industry for their expertise and influence, but it is much less common because public sector salaries and bonuses can rarely compete with their private counterparts.

One of the most obvious and important examples of the interpenetration of the state and corporations is the financial support that the state so often gives to markets, particularly when they fail. The English economist John Maynard Keynes considered it to be one of the essential functions of government to stabilise the cyclical excesses and deficiencies of imperfect markets and optimise economic conditions through active state intervention. This view became orthodoxy in the advanced economies of the West after World War Two. In the financial crisis of 2008, the UK government rescued several of Britain's insolvent private banks with an emergency £850 billion bailout.[9] By 2009 the government had provided them with loans, share purchases and guarantees amounting to £1.162 trillion. The US government did much the same with its Emergency Economic Stabilisation Act, which created a $700 billion Troubled Asset

Relief Program (TARP) to bail out the country's failing private banks and investment firms. The German federal government bailed out many of the country's failing regional banks, as did the government in France, which pumped hundreds of billions of euros into its banks to save them from collapse.

No one seriously questions the existence of a significant 'State–Corporate Nexus' today. But the emergence in the twentieth century of a welfare state to replace the classical state shows the limits to Marx's extreme view of the state as nothing but a weapon in the hands of the ruling class to control and coerce the toiling multitudes. Unlike Lasalle, he never imagined a future state that would support the health and well-being of its citizens, something he believed would have to await the advent of a communist society when the state had disappeared altogether.

The Welfare State

Just as many Western states were expanding and refining their coercive and destructive powers thanks to advances in technology, they were also beginning to intervene to curb the naked inhumanity of early industrial capitalism. These two contradictory tendencies grew in tandem, reflecting the two faces of state power, one positive and one negative. In Britain humanitarian concerns about the plight of the working poor grew during the nineteenth century and began to influence public policy. The UK then had the most advanced industrial economy in the world, which had been pretty much left alone by the government, with truly appalling consequences for much of the population. Many writers, politicians, public moralists, social critics and religious figures worried about the 'Condition of England Question', as it was labelled by the writer Thomas Carlyle. The expression referred to the mounting concern about the dehumanising effects of the new industrial system on workers, many of whom were children. He warned that it was turning people into soulless machines and had reduced the lives of millions to drudgery, poverty and ugliness.

Although Carlyle's criticisms influenced a generation of Victorian intellectuals, it was the popular novels of Charles Dickens that raised the hellishness of industrial England to a national scandal. Karl Marx, who spent most of his life in London, credited the great Victorian novelists such Dickens, William Makepeace Thackeray and Charlotte Brontë with having 'issued to the world more political and social truths than have been uttered by all the professional politicians, publicists and moralists put together'.[10] This was the beginning of what would gradually develop into a revolutionary transformation of the modern understanding of the purposes of the state over the next century.

Early reforms in Britain initially focused on improving working conditions in factories. One of the first of these, the

Cotton Mills Act of 1819, banned children under the age of nine from working in a cotton mill and limited the working day for those under sixteen to twelve hours. A long series of other 'Factory Acts' followed throughout the nineteenth and twentieth centuries, gradually reducing the working day and working week, and establishing a system of elementary education in factory schools funded by the government. The welfare of people beyond this was left mainly to churches, which provided most of the limited education and charity that existed then for the general population.

It wasn't until the late nineteenth century that the first steps towards the establishment of the modern welfare state were tentatively taken. Until then, states had principally concerned themselves with maintaining peace internally and promoting the national interest abroad, often by making war. It was Otto von Bismarck, the conservative 'Iron Chancellor' of the newly unified German Reich, who led the way, encouraged by the socialist Lasalle, whom he read and knew personally. In the early 1880s he supported a novel programme of social legislation that he referred to as 'practical Christianity'. An example is the Old Age and Disability Insurance Law (1889), which provided an annuity for retired workers when they reached the age of seventy, although it is doubtful many made it that far after a life of toil in the nineteenth century. Also included in this plan was sickness insurance, accident insurance and disability insurance. Germany's example inspired similar policies in other European countries, such as France. In the UK workmen's compensation was introduced in 1893, old age pensions in 1908 and unemployment insurance in 1911.

A major part of Bismarck's motive in proposing reforms in Germany was to win the support of ordinary workers to the new state that he had just established in 1871. Also, he was eager to discourage them from supporting the Social Democratic Party, which had recently been founded by Lassalle. It was one of the first of many socialist and social democratic parties that were formed at the end of the nineteenth and early twentieth centuries in the West, although some working-class political movements such as Chartism in England had existed for decades by then. These parties of the left proposed radical reforms intended to improve the condition of the working poor and reduce inequality. Their membership often overlapped with trade unions that also surged in number and size in the late nineteenth century to press for improvements to working conditions.

The industrial democracies of the West in the first half of the twentieth century saw the gradual emergence of what we now call the welfare state, building on these early reforms to replace the classical state. States not only asserted themselves more and more forcefully in the market but made greater provision for the health and well-being of their citizens. Whereas the earlier classical liberal state was essentially negative, protecting lives and property, the welfare state of the twentieth century was an active and positive state that had taken on the role of promoting health, education, welfare and the public good.

The stock market crash in 1929 greatly accelerated this slow transformation of the state. It was the most serious crisis of capitalism in its history till then, leading governments of almost all political hues to intervene in markets to an unprecedented extent. Franklin Roosevelt, first elected president of the United States in 1933, implemented his ambitious 'New Deal' programme of public works, financial regulation and social assistance to address the disastrous effects of this great economic crisis. Canada's Conservative prime minister R. B. Bennett followed his example and belatedly instituted his country's own New Deal. After gaining power in 1933 the Nazis expanded the welfare state that Bismarck had begun in Germany. In Scandinavia the corporatist 'Nordic model' of capitalism involving cooperation between labour and capital was adopted in the 1930s.

Even 'New Liberals' of the twentieth century, whose classical nineteenth-century ancestors had defended limited states and free markets, moved in these years to embrace a much more active role for states in the economic life of nations. This was expressed most clearly in Britain in the seminal 1942 Beveridge Report, recommending a universal system of social security and the creation of a publicly funded national health system. The report was written by a Liberal Party economist and adopted after the war by the Labour government of

Clement Attlee. The gradual construction of a comprehensive cradle-to-the-grave welfare state was completed in the aftermath of World War Two, ensuring that all citizens were provided with a full range of benefits either directly by the state or funded by it, with the notable exception of healthcare in the US. It was the culmination of a process that had taken a century and its centrepiece in Britain was the National Health Service.

The history of education followed the same basic pattern over roughly the same period as healthcare during the century prior to 1950, by which time free, universal, compulsory public schooling was the norm in all developed and many developing countries. This was almost entirely an achievement of the state, which gradually wrested control of what education there was from religious institutions, which had provided it for some children. But the vast majority of people received little or no formal education even from churches or charities until late in the nineteenth century. By a steady series of enactments, governments gradually took over the funding of education from other institutions and extended it to groups who had hitherto never had access to any. As with healthcare, the wealthy had always paid for their own education, either by hiring private tutors or by sending their children to fee-paying schools. For the rest there was some minimal religious instruction, charitable education or, in most cases, nothing. Within a century mass public education in state-run schools up to the age of sixteen was standard across the Western world. The exponential rise in rates of literacy and numeracy that began in the late nineteenth century reflects this state-led expansion in popular education.[11]

Controlling Capitalism

The postwar welfare state was intended to address the many deficiencies and injustices of capitalist markets (so-called 'externalities', in the clinical language of economists) so that everyone would be provided with the most basic human needs. It acts as a 'social safety net' to catch those who fall out of the market through illness or unemployment or who are unable to fully provide for themselves even in work. But the expanding role of the state in the twentieth century did not stop with welfare. Many Western countries also took private businesses into public ownership after World War Two. This was particularly so in key sectors of the economy such as heavy industry, transportation, telecommunications and natural resources (gas, oil and minerals), which were considered strategically important and many of which are natural monopolies. This was also the time when many central banks and railways were nationalised, as in Argentina, Britain and France. Despite the government being virtually bankrupt, Britain's coal, iron, steel, gas and electricity industries were nationalised immediately after World War Two, as was most of the transportation system. By the time this initial wave of nationalisations had petered out in 1951, when the Labour government of Clement Attlee lost power, the UK public sector employed four million people – 18 per cent of the workforce.[12]

A second wave of nationalisations followed under UK Labour governments in the 1970s, when Rolls-Royce, British Petroleum, British Leyland Motors, British Aerospace and Post Office Telecommunications were all taken into public owner-ship. Between 1950 and 1980 public expenditure as a share of GDP rose in the UK from 32 per cent to 45 per cent, as the scope of direct government involvement in the economy expanded continuously. The UK government also renational-ised the country's privatised rail infrastructure when it went bankrupt in 2003 and acquired a majority share in several failing banks in 2008–9 during the financial crisis, including the Royal Bank of Scotland, then one of the largest banks in the world.

France went even further than Britain after the war, with the government taking ownership of most major utilities, including the nuclear power industry. By 1946 the French state directly controlled 98 per cent of coal production, 95 per cent of electricity, 58 per cent of the banking sector, 38 per cent of automobile production and 15 per cent of total GDP.[13] A central Commissariat général du Plan was established in 1946 to draft five-year plans for the French economy. This *dirigiste* system in which the state plays a leading role in directing the French economy led to what later became known as *les Trente Glorieuses* (the 'thirty glorious years'), when high economic growth and low unemployment lasted for three decades (1945–75). One crucial difference between France and Britain at the time is that France nationalised many of its private banks, which gave its state great power over the allocation of funding to private businesses.[14] Apart from the Bank of England, the UK government left the country's banking sector in private hands, which proved to be a serious mistake. Unlike France, it restricted its nationalised industries' access to private capital, fearing that it would give them a competitive edge over their private competitors by using it to improve obsolete infrastructure and undertake research and development. This left many of them underfunded and unprofitable, which later advocates of privatisation would use to support their case that public ownership is a sure path to poor service and inefficiency compared to the private sector.

The election of a Socialist government under President François Mitterrand in 1981 led to a second, sweeping wave of nationalisations in France. The government took over the major industrial groups of CGE, Pechiney, Rhône-Poulenc, Saint-Gobain and Thomson; defence manufacturers Dassault-Breguet and Matra; steel giants Usinor and Sacilor; computer companies Bull and ITT France; the pharmaceutical lab Roussel UCLAF; and the country's thirty-six biggest private banks. Although the French government sold off many of these public companies in the 1990s, by 2006 it still controlled ninety of them directly (representing 3.7 per cent of total employment) and 755 indirectly.[15]

Many governments in South and Central America acquired a broad range of utilities and industries in the twentieth century as a means of fostering domestic industrial development and offsetting the dominance of foreign companies looking to exploit the region's vast natural resources. For example, the Brazilian president Getúlio Dornelles Vargas nationalised his country's steel industry in 1941 and oil in 1953. This was followed by another phase of nationalisations in the late 1960s and 1970s, when aircraft manufacturer Embraer, telecom monopoly Telebrás, and Nuclebrás all became state-owned enterprises (SOEs). In the 1930s President Lázaro Cárdenas nationalised Mexico's oil, electricity and railways, with a second wave of nationalisations following in the 1960s and 1970s. The 'Pink Tide' of left-wing governments elected in the region in the early twenty-first century led to a new wave of nationalisations there. Bolivian president Evo Morales nationalised the telecommunications firm Entel, the country's main hydroelectric plant and the power grid operator TDE. In Venezuela President Hugo Chávez nationalised some foreign businesses operating in the country, including retail shops and cement companies. Argentina's President Cristina Kirchner nationalised the nation's largest energy firm, YPF, and the country's private pension funds.

By contrast, there has been relatively little direct public ownership of industry and resources in Sweden, Australia and

Canada, although the latter created several state-owned, independently operated 'Crown Corporations', including the Canadian National Railway (1919), the Bank of Canada (1935), the Canadian Broadcasting Corporation (1936), the National Film Board (1939) and Air Canada (1937). Although the Swedish government nationalised the country's bankrupt shipbuilding industry in the 1970s, this was an exception to the norm in that country, which has followed the corporatist 'Nordic model'. This involves a 'grand compromise' between capital and labour where most businesses remain in private hands but there is a comprehensive welfare state and collective bargaining between the state, trade unions and industry. Labor prime minister Ben Chifley's attempt to nationalise Australia's banking system in 1947 was thwarted in the courts following an aggressive and well-funded campaign against the proposal by the country's powerful banks.

While many developing economies in postwar East Asia, such as South Korea, Taiwan, Japan and Singapore, did not nationalise businesses to the same degree as the industrial West, they adopted a system of 'developmental capitalism' where powerful state ministries play a pivotal role in planning and directing their national economies, often by investing in and carefully regulating private companies. Like the Soviet Union, Communist China and Cuba were special cases during these decades since the state in those countries already owned all of the means of production.

The Allies imposed market regulation on Germany and Japan after they were defeated in World War Two. There had previously been no antitrust legislation in Japan, so General Douglas MacArthur forced its government to enact the Antimonopoly Act in 1947, which is still the country's fundamental competition law. Today the Japanese Fair Trade Commission and the German Federal Cartel Office (*Bundeskartellamt*) exist to prevent monopolies forming in their respective countries.

With this huge expansion in government involvement in economies all over the world, by the 1970s public enterprise accounted for an average of 13.5 per cent of capital formation in countries for which investment figures are available, according to a broad statistical comparison carried out by the IMF.[16]

The United States followed a different path, opting for public regulation of the market over public ownership. There was some temporary nationalisation of industry, but it was exceptional. For example, the US Federal government nationalised railroads, telegraph lines and the arms and ammunition manufacturer Smith and Wesson during World War One as a temporary wartime measure but very quickly returned them to private ownership after the war. It did the same in World War Two for the same reason. President Harry Truman's attempted nationalisation of the US steel industry in 1952 to avert a strike that he claimed threatened the war effort in Korea was ruled unconstitutional by the Supreme Court.

The general trend towards increasing government regulation of businesses began in the US during the 'great merger movement' in the late nineteenth century, the age of the 'robber barons', with the ominous growth of monopolies and cartels such as John D. Rockefeller's mammoth Standard Oil Company, one of the world's first multinational corporations. In 1911 the US Supreme Court ordered it to be broken up into thirty-four separate companies for violating the Sherman Act (1890), the first of many laws passed to prevent actions that would 'substantially lessen competition' in the marketplace such as the creation of trusts, which were legal instruments used by businesses to combine smaller companies into a single monopoly, as happened to the hundreds of small short-line railroads that existed in the US at the time.

This early pioneering 'antitrust' legislation, enacted during the 'Progressive Era' in the United States when the public mood was increasingly hostile to big business, inspired similar regulations in other countries, such as Canada and in Europe. It inaugurated a golden age of controlled capitalism in the US that lasted, more or less, until the 1970s. The US Department of Justice was empowered by this legislation to sue businesses in the courts for deliberately engaging in anticompetitive practices, although it allowed 'innocent monopolies' that were not a consequence of a deliberate effort to undermine competition. The Clayton Antitrust Act (1914) was an attempt to plug the many holes in the Sherman Act, as were the Robinson–Patman Act (1936), prohibiting anticompetitive practices by producers, and the Celler–Kefauver Act (1950), which strengthened the government's power to prevent mergers that would reduce competition.

The US government also set up several agencies in the early part of the twentieth century, such as the Federal Trade Commission (1914), the Federal Deposit Insurance Corporation (1933) and the Securities and Exchange Commission (1934), to oversee business conduct and set and impose standards, particularly in financial markets. The FDIC was created by the same Banking Act that included the 'Glass–Steagall' provisions crucially separating commercial and investment banking, the latter of which had been blamed for encouraging rash speculation that contributed to the Wall Street crash of 1929. These were later gradually whittled down, overridden and rescinded in the 1990s, contributing to another period of frenzied speculation and irresponsible investment that culminated in the financial crisis of 2008.

With all these rules and regulations at its disposal, the US government has periodically taken companies to court to break up private monopolies. In the 1990s the Federal Department of Justice sued Microsoft under the Sherman Act for its monopoly position in the personal computer market. The court found against Microsoft and ordered it to be broken into two. After an appeal the Department of Justice reached an out-of-court settlement with the company, which is now ranked twenty-first on the 2020 Fortune 500 list of the largest firms in the US by total revenue. Even the Reagan administration successfully used the Sherman Act to break up the telephone monopoly AT&T into several regional operating companies in 1982. As of 2020, AT&T was ranked ninth on the Fortune 500 list. In 2020 the Department of Justice filed an antitrust lawsuit against Google for allegedly monopolising web searches by paying Apple between $8 billion and $12 billion to be the default search engine on iPhones. It is possible that the US government will one day do the same to social media companies such as Twitter and Facebook.

The United States was ahead of most countries in setting up a system of rules and regulations to control private enterprise and most states have followed their lead. In Britain a whole series of laws were enacted over many years to empower the government to prevent monopolies and to regulate the economy, starting with the Monopolies and Restrictive Practices (Inquiry and Control) Act (1948), followed by the Restrictive Trade Practices Act (1956), the Monopolies and Mergers Act (1965), the Monopolies and Restrictive Trade Practices Act (1969), the UK Competition Act (1998), the Enterprise Act (2002) and the Enterprise and Regulatory Reform Act (2013). Regulatory agencies such as the UK Competition and Markets Authority, the Office of Fair Trading, the Competition Commission and the Financial Conduct Authority were also set up by successive governments to control capitalism's excesses through regulation. Most countries today have a statutory body empowered to protect competition, such as France's Autorité de la concurrence, Italy's Autorità Garante della Concorrenza e del Mercato, and Australia's Competition and Consumer Commission.

The state brings out the best and the worst in us. It is worth remembering that the twentieth-century welfare state that has done so much to lift up the masses is also a warfare state that has sent many of them to their deaths. The earlier classical state did less to help its citizens than we do, but it didn't fight total wars of the kind experienced in the first half of the twentieth century either. That is principally because it lacked the technological means to do so. Advances in science and increased prosperity have greatly enhanced the power and scope of the state, for better and for worse. It has greatly enhanced the power of many other agencies as well, including terrorists, private corporations, pirates and criminal organisations. States claim a monopoly on the legitimate use of violence, but they do not possess it in practice. And states do not just use violence; they often protect us from it too. States grew out of the breakdown of the medieval world as a means of imposing order on chaos. Failed states and weak states today are as much of a threat to most people as strong, overbearing states. So, relative to the past, states are stronger in many ways, but relative to other powers today, they are weaker than they were, and that is not good news for many ordinary people.

2

PRIVATE GOOD, PUBLIC BAD

The global neoliberal revolution that British prime minister Margaret Thatcher took credit for was conceived and instigated by people who are today confusingly called 'conservative'. That would make her a 'neoliberal conservative revolutionary', which shows how meaningless our antiquated political vocabulary has become. A century earlier she would have fitted very comfortably in the ranks of Victorian classical liberals, next to Herbert Spencer and Richard Cobden. Thatcher's twentieth-century intellectual hero, the Austrian economist Friedrich Hayek, wrote a very sensible essay on 'Why I am Not a Conservative', a postscript to one of her favourite books, *The Constitution of Liberty* (1960). In it he describes himself as a liberal in the nineteenth-century sense, although his preferred label is 'Old Whig' – 'with the stress on the "old"'.

Whether we should call Thatcher a 'conservative', 'neoconservative', 'classical liberal' or 'neoliberal' is debatable, and perhaps ultimately rather pointless, but there can be no doubt that she was a revolutionary. When she became a Conservative Member of Parliament in 1959, neoliberal ideas and policies favouring limited government involvement in the economy were very far from dominant. Thatcher saw the world as gripped by a 'collectivist' ideology and ruinous economic policies that she made it her mission to overturn. She agreed with Hayek when he said that 'there is in the present world very little reason for the liberal to wish to preserve things as they are. It would seem to the liberal, indeed, that what is most urgently needed in most parts of the world is a thorough sweeping away of the obstacle to free growth.'[1] This radical view was shared by Thatcher's friend and fellow believer in 'the magic of the marketplace', US president Ronald Reagan, who also included Hayek among the writers who had most influenced his own opinions about politics and economics.

Before the 'neoliberal' revolution began, it first won a battle of ideas, as most revolutions do. Like Soviet Communism, neoliberalism was a revolutionary intellectual movement before it became a political and economic success. This can be seen in the similarity of the relationship between the intellectual Hayek and the politician Thatcher, on the one hand, and Marx and Lenin, on the other, although the latter two never met whereas the first two did. Soon after she became leader of her party and began her 'crusade' (her word) for 'popular capitalism' (also her words), a meeting between the future prime minister and the famous economist was held at the Institute of Economic Affairs in London, a neoliberal think-tank that had been set up on Hayek's advice to spread the gospel about the glories of free market capitalism.

Hayek was at the intellectual centre of this movement. He had attended the Walter Lippmann conference in Paris in August 1938 which brought together a small group of businessmen, economists and politicians to form a 'neoliberalist offensive' against the planned economy when socialism and fascism were both ascendant in Europe and liberalism was deeply unfashionable. Hayek was also one of the founders of the Mont Pelerin Society, whose first president he became. It was devoted to studying and promoting neoliberal policies, particularly in opposition to the then-dominant ideas of John Maynard Keynes in the West and Karl Marx in the East. It became one of many such bodies established to promote free market fundamentalism, such as the Heritage Foundation, the Institute of Economic Affairs and the Adam Smith Institute. Hayek spent the 1950s as a professor at the University of Chicago, which was a hub of free market economics and anti-statist politics (the 'Chicago School'). It was there that he finished *The Constitution of Liberty* which so impressed his young admirer, Margaret Thatcher. The award of a Nobel Prize in Economics to Hayek in 1974 was an unmistakable sign of how much neoliberal ideas had gained in acceptability and influence by then. The Cold War between the capitalist West and the communist East was the broad context within which neoliberal ideas germinated as Thatcher's own political and economic views developed.

The University of Chicago was also the academic home of the economist Milton Friedman, who won the Nobel Prize two years after Hayek, further evidence of the intellectual success of the neoliberal revolution in ideas which preceded its political and economic revolution. In 1988 Reagan awarded Friedman the Presidential Medal of Freedom, his nation's highest civilian honour, which was conferred on Hayek three years later. The influence of Friedman's economic ideas is difficult to exaggerate and rivals that of Hayek. When Friedman died in 2006, Harvard president Lawrence Summers, a Democrat, quipped that 'we are now all Friedmanites', a joke about Friedman's earlier comment that 'we are all Keynesians now', which Richard Nixon later used. Far from reversing the neoliberal revolution begun in Britain by the Conservatives and in the US by the Republicans, their successors on the political left (men like Bill Clinton, Tony Blair and Gerhard Schröder) consolidated and often expanded it, while dropping or muting the strident nationalism and social conservatism of Thatcher and Reagan. By 2000 the neoliberal revolution had become the neoliberal status quo. Only then was it really 'conservative', as revolutions become as soon as they are victorious.

Selling the State

The policy of 'privatisation' is a key component of the neoliberal effort to 'roll back the frontiers of the state', as Thatcher put it, in order to promote economic growth and political freedom. It involves selling off state-owned industries to the private sector and amounts to a reversal of the approach widely adopted in the aftermath of World War Two when major parts of the national economies of many countries were taken into public ownership.

The policy is based on an assumption that the private sector is inherently more efficient and rational at producing goods and services than states are, a belief that became an article of faith for many despite the absence of supporting evidence. Privatisation also assumes that it is ethically preferable for such goods and services to be freely transacted in lightly regulated markets than controlled and allocated by states. It is a deliberate attempt to 'spread the nation's wealth', as Thatcher expressed it, by shifting wealth and power from the public realm to the private. She called this a 'property owning democracy' in which ordinary people would be able to buy their own homes and purchase shares in denationalised industries that would be sold to whoever could afford them. As we shall see, all of these assumptions are highly questionable, if not demonstrably false.

In Britain it was actually the Labour government of Prime Minister James Callaghan that took the first, tentative step in the direction of neoliberalism in 1976. In the face of the 'twin evils of unemployment and inflation', the reduction of which was then the Labour government's 'first priority', Callaghan cut government spending. While this was not a full-blown assault on the postwar Keynesian consensus, it was an important departure from it, particularly as it came from a Labour government. But it did not extend to the privatisation of nationalised industries, which only began with Thatcher's election in 1979.

Margaret Thatcher saw herself as a pioneer of privatisation, not just in Britain but around the world. At first, though, she was cautious. In 1977 she received the final, confidential report of the Conservative Party's 'Nationalised Industries Policy Group' that had been chaired by the Tory MP Nicholas Ridley, a true believer in her free market revolution. It set out a plan for 'denationalisation' of Britain's public-owned businesses 'by stealth' rather than by means of a 'frontal attack'. If elected, the report argued, a Conservative government should 'edge them back into the private sector', first by introducing market measures such as financial incentives for managers and a required rate of return on capital before 'fragmentation' of the industries into smaller units, when they would be sold off to private investors. The report's frequent references to the greater 'efficiency' of the private sector over the public, dominated as it is by 'the bureaucratic mind', provides the policy's principal justification.

The centrepiece of 'Thatcherism' during her first government (1979–83) was the policy of right-to-buy. When she became prime minister in 1979 a third of all homes in the UK were rented from the state.[2] The Housing Act of 1980 gave most of these renters the right to buy their home from their local authority at a considerable discount below their market value; previously, the authority's permission had been required. The new law was presented to Parliament by the environment secretary Michael Heseltine, who declared that it 'lays the foundations for one of the most important social revolutions of this century'. At first the policy was angrily opposed by the Labour Party, although it later sheepishly accepted it.

Over two million council homes were sold in Britain between 1979 and 1996 and, at first, home ownership increased from 55 per cent of the population in 1980 to a peak of 70.9 per cent in 2003. But then it began to decline, falling to 62.9 per cent in 2015–16, the lowest level in three decades. And the trend is continuing downwards. Meanwhile, the number of people renting has increased to 4.5 million households, its highest level in absolute numbers since 1961. Many who bought their council flats later sold them to investors, who rented them out at much higher prices. The stock of 'social housing' available to rent to those on low incomes who cannot afford private market rates has shrunk considerably. Millions of council properties were sold off under right-to-buy, leading to a serious housing shortage and long and growing waiting lists that continue to this day.[3]

The other key plank of Thatcher's policy of 'popular capitalism' was selling off nationalised industries to private investors to 'spread the nation's wealth'. This did not begin in a big way until the Conservatives were re-elected in 1983 with a much-increased parliamentary majority. She reasoned that, because 'state planners do not have to suffer the consequences of their mistakes', as they were backed up by taxpayers, the government should stick to the business of governing and let private businesses do what they do best. That the many private, 'too-big-to-fail' businesses are effectively guaranteed by taxpayers if they fail, as happened in 2008, appears not to have occurred to Prime Minister Thatcher. Nor did the possibility that, far from 'spreading the nation's wealth', it would actually increase its concentration in the hands of those who were already very well off, the very opposite of its declared purpose and one of its principal justifications.

And so began the great sell-off. Britoil, British Telecom, Sealink Ferries, British Petroleum, British Aerospace, British Gas, Rolls-Royce Aircraft Engines, the Rover Group, British Steel, the British Airports Authority and regional water authorities were all transferred to private ownership during Margaret Thatcher's eleven years as prime minister, as she had promised. And they were sold very cheaply too. One of the most controversial privatisations was British Rail, begun in 1994 under Thatcher's successor John Major. It had been nationalised in 1948 and was back in private hands by

1997. The Labour Party, which was in power for a decade with back-to-back majority governments from 1997 to 2010, at first strenuously objected to this policy but never actually renationalised any Conservative privatisations.

Margaret Thatcher's 'popular capitalism' never materialised. Privatisation did not 'spread the wealth'. Instead, it narrowed it even further. Prior to her election in 1979, individuals owned around 40 per cent of shares in UK companies. When she died in 2013 it was just 12 per cent.[4] The policy also resulted in a large increase in foreign ownership in the UK, a trend that is particularly strong in privatised water and energy companies.[5] How Thatcher reconciled this with her nationalistic views remains a mystery, at least to me, and perhaps it did to her as well.

Like Britain, France undertook extensive nationalisation of its industries after World War Two. And, also like its neighbour, it started selling them off in the 1980s. This is surprising given the strong tradition of statism in France and its lack of popular support for neoliberal ideas, which are widely seen as an essentially Anglo-Saxon form of barbarism and therefore unsuitable for the world's most civilised nation. In fact, when the Socialist leader François Mitterrand was elected to the presidency in 1981 he immediately launched a new wave of nationalisations. He was still president in 1986 when his party lost control of the French parliament. This led to a brief period of political power-sharing ('cohabitation', as it is called in

France) with conservative Gaullist prime minister Jacques Chirac that lasted for two years. Chirac used this opportunity to begin the first wave of French privatisations, which included the car manufacturer Renault, CGE, Saint-Gobain, Matra and the bank Société Générale.

Another period of political 'cohabitation' in the mid-1990s was the occasion for another round of state sell-offs, including Elf Aquitaine, Rhône-Poulenc, Bull, Pechiney and Usinor-Sacilor. This process did not end when the Socialist leader Lionel Jospin became French prime minister in 1997, 'cohabiting' with President Chirac. Jospin privatised Crédit Lyonnais and sold minority shares in Aérospatiale, Air France and the largest individual sale of a public company in France at the time: France Télécom. His successors carried on this new, bipartisan privatisation policy. What may have been instinctively unpalatable to ordinary French citizens was apparently very much to the taste of their political elites on both sides.

Spanish governments of left and right privatised 134 state-owned businesses between 1985 and 2005. Most of this (60 per cent) occurred while the Spanish Socialist Party (PSOE) was in power. The process included strategic industries such as telecommunications, energy, transportation and banking. Part of the reason for such sweeping privatisation was to reduce public debt to comply with the EU's Maastricht Treaty that was concluded in 1992. By selling off state enterprises the government cut the public payroll and pocketed large one-off cash windfalls to meet the EU's requirements. But in doing so it lost public control over many important Spanish businesses and industries.

In the 1990s Italy partially privatised its state-owned Eni oil and gas firm, the state telephone monopoly, Enel electric power company and Autrostrade, which owned and operated toll roads and motorways. Wisely, it held on to some shares in each, giving it limited control over these partly private businesses. Unwisely, it decentralised its national healthcare system in 1997, giving regions considerable autonomy on how to spend funding provided centrally by Rome. Some regional governments encouraged public–private competition for these public funds in their areas, believing competition would be healthy for healthcare. It wasn't. Private clinics boomed while public hospitals struggled in this market environment, distorting healthcare priorities and causing underfunding in key areas. This may have exacerbated the rapid spread of the Coronavirus in hotspots of northern Italy in 2020 that led to many deaths, at least according to some reports.

A frenzy of selling swept across South and Central America in the 1990s, much of it a consequence of intense pressure applied to governments in the developing world by neoliberal true believers at international agencies like the International Monetary Fund and the World Bank. Austerity, privatisation and tariff reductions were routinely demanded in return for loans, which typically come with a host of such conditions.

The Mexican government sold off the overwhelming majority of its publicly owned companies in a remarkably short period of time. A 'Disincorporation Unit' was established to coordinate the process which, by the mid-1990s, had reduced state-owned enterprises from over a thousand in 1983 to just eighty.[6] No pressure was needed to induce Argentina's President Carlos Menem to join the stampede to sell. He was already convinced and made privatisation a key component of the pro-market policies he implemented in his country in the 1990s. Among the principal beneficiaries of this process were foreign investors, particularly from the United States. A similar pattern of economic liberalisation and mass privatisation occurred in Peru, especially under President Alberto Fujimori, and in Brazil.

The most brutal form of privatisation occurred in Russia after the collapse of the Soviet system in 1989. Having owned the entire industrial economy under communism, the new Russian state found itself with vast numbers of antiquated and inefficient industries it was desperate to transfer to private hands as quickly (and cheaply) as possible. It chose a controversial voucher privatisation scheme for doing this, supervised by a government agency under Anatoly Chubais, who had originally criticised this approach but later conveniently (to him) changed his mind about it. Chubais surrounded himself with a cabal of American economic advisors, many from the Harvard Institute for International Development, who shared his evangelical devotion to free market fundamentalism and were committed to neoliberal 'shock therapy' for post-communist Russia. Citizens were issued with freely tradeable vouchers by President Boris Yeltsin's government which they could use in auctions of shares of privatising enterprises. The outcome of this rash and flawed process, dubbed 'piratisation' and 'briberisation' by some, was a disaster for ordinary Russians. When the privatisation music stopped, a few well-placed oligarchs were billionaires holding many of the shares in the newly privatised industries, while most Russians were left empty-handed. Years of terrible hardship followed.[7] Between 1990 and 1999, industrial production plunged by 60 per cent, GDP by 54 per cent and poverty shot up from 2 per cent to over 23 per cent. Not an auspicious introduction to capitalism after seven decades of communism.

Privatisation has even occurred at the international level. Increasingly, national governments and domestic bodies have delegated regulatory authority to international private-sector organisations to set and impose their own standards. In their study of this subject, Tim Büthe and Walter Mattli describe the 2008 decision of the Securities and Exchange Commission (SEC), the US financial market regulator, to switch from the US Generally Accepted Accounting Principles (GAAP) to International Financial Reporting Standards (IFRS) as 'momentous'. It represents a significant victory for private rule-making in the political battles over international regulation. Now, the International Organisation for Standardisation (ISO) and International Electrotechnical Commission (IEC) 'jointly account for about 85 per cent of all international product standards'.[8] Such private-sector regulation is not subject to the same degree of public accountability and critical oversight as national government regulation in democratic states. This means they will be more likely to set standards that promote industry interests at the expense of public interests.

One country that did not join in the great sell-off was the United States because, as we saw in the last chapter, there had been relatively little nationalisation to begin with. The same is true of Sweden, where there was no widespread state ownership. There were few state-owned 'Crown Corporations' in Canada but its government still sold off the strategically vital oil company Petro-Canada, the Canadian National Railway and Air Canada in the 1980s and 1990s. Australia was in a similar position, with relatively few state-owned enterprises, yet governments on both sides privatised much of what there was in public hands, including Qantas Airlines, telecommunications firm Telstra, the pharmaceutical company Commonwealth Serum Laboratories and the Commonwealth Bank of Australia.

Privatisation does not, in itself, necessarily lead to reduced government spending, which remains quite high in most OECD countries as a percentage of GDP, ranging from 24.5 per cent in Ireland to 55.3 per cent in France in 2019. In 1995 it was 38.1 per cent in the US, 41 per cent in Britain, 45.2 per cent in Germany and 45.2 per cent averaged across all OECD countries, down slightly from 47.7 per cent.[9] So public spending still accounts for a substantial portion of the national economy of most developed countries, around 40 per cent, mainly to fund the cost of public healthcare, education and welfare. It was around 10 per cent in 1900, when many of these services were not provided by states. In Britain, government ownership of industry fell sharply from 9 per cent to 4 per cent under Thatcher but the economic size of the state overall remained fairly constant.[10] Even in the US, government spending as a proportion of GDP was around 38 per cent in 2020.[11] Privatisation doesn't really reduce government spending much, if at all, over the long term, particularly if the newly privatised firms axe jobs, as they often do, thereby adding to the number of people in need of government support. It just reduces, or removes entirely, direct state involvement in important sectors of the economy, which are sold to private, profit-seeking investors. The role and importance of the state in the economic life of a nation is not simply a matter of its size. Much also depends on what it does, and in the West it has been doing less and less in the economy except when it periodically bails out failing banks and businesses.

Margaret Thatcher was not exaggerating when she triumphantly declared to her party in 1986 that

So popular is our policy that it's being taken up all round the world. From France to the Philippines, from Jamaica to

Japan, from Malaysia to Mexico, from Sri Lanka to Singapore, privatisation is on the move. There's even a special Oriental version in China. The policies we have pioneered are catching on in country after country. We Conservatives believe in popular capitalism – believe in a property-owning democracy – and it works![12]

She was only wrong about the very last bit, unless she meant that it works for those who are already rich.

Outsourcing the State

Where states have not actually sold off their assets or industries, they have often hired private companies to deliver services to the government or the public after a process of competitive tendering. Such 'outsourcing' of work to the private sector has become a widespread practice now employed across virtually the entire range of government activities. The justification for this marketisation of public services is purported cost-saving, as it is assumed private businesses are better able to provide services quickly and more cheaply than outdated, sclerotic government bureaucracies.

Not surprisingly, such outsourcing of government activity began on a large scale in Britain under Margaret Thatcher, whose faith in the efficiency and cost-effectiveness of private enterprise was as dogmatic as it was unbounded. Equally unsurprising is that it not only continued under Labour governments but was greatly extended by them. By 2018–19, more than a third of all public spending (equivalent to £292 billion) was being spent on goods, works and services from private firms.[13] From peripheral activities such as waste collection and IT support it was rapidly extended to areas once considered integral to the core purposes of the state, such as prisons, national defence, hospitals and many front-line public services. Thirteen of the 121 prisons in England and Wales are now run by the private sector, encompassing 19 per cent of the prison population, partly to cut costs because private prisons usually pay their staff less than their public counterparts. For a time the UK Ministry of Justice even contracted out the supervision of medium- and low-risk offenders released from prison on probation, although this was ended a few years later in response to public unease. In 2014 the government also abandoned plans to expand outsourcing to child protection services, given its sensitivity.

Probably the most controversial area of government activity to be outsourced in Britain is the National Health Service. In 2018–19 just over 7 per cent of its budget in England was being spent on the purchase of private-sector goods and services of various kinds, a very conservative estimate thought by many experts to significantly understate the actual level.[14] This policy was instituted by Thatcher, who legally required NHS hospitals to field competitive bids from the private sector for many of its services. There are now dozens of companies working for the NHS, such as Virgin Care (part of the Virgin Group), Ramsay Health Care, Serco and Capita. Two of the NHS's largest private suppliers (Carillion and Interserve) entered liquidation in 2018 and 2019. Many have been involved in controversies over cost-cutting, overcharging, incompetence and fraud.

Government outsourcing to 'independent service providers' is now so extensive and lucrative that it has become big business. Some corporations like the outsourcing giant Serco, which runs part of the NHS's extremely expensive and largely ineffective Covid-19 Test and Trace system, exist solely to provide government services for a profit, which they do all over the world. They operate trains, ferries, buses, city metros, monorails, road speed cameras, prisons, young offender institutions, immigration control centres, Royal Navy fleet support, air traffic control services, facilities management services at hospitals, local authority leisure centres (gyms, swimming pools, sports facilities), waste collection, parking meter regulations (in Chicago), driving test examination centres (in Ontario) and the US patenting system.

London-based firm Capita is another large international outsourcing company, half of whose business derives from the public sector. Although most of its contracts are in the UK, it also has operations in Europe, Africa and Asia. Its work for the NHS, the British Army and the Royal Navy, among others, has often been highly controversial owing to a litany of problems leading to the termination or non-renewal of many of its contracts.[15]

G4S is the world's largest private security company (by revenues), which sells its services in ninety countries, including to many governments. It has expanded very aggressively, buying up companies all over the world since it was formed in 2004 as an amalgamation of Group 4 and Falck. It is perhaps best known today for the fiasco of the 2012 London Olympics. G4S signed a £284 million contract with the UK government to provide security for the Games. This required them to train almost fourteen thousand guards, but they had to report to the government just two weeks before the opening of the Olympics that they had fallen short by several thousand. The police and the army (i.e. the state) had to be brought in to fill the huge security gap and many of those who had been 'trained' had little idea of what they were doing or where they were supposed to be.[16]

The French multinational IT service and consulting firm Atos is another of the UK government's biggest outsourcing suppliers, with contracts to provide services to NHS Scotland, the Home Office, the Welsh government, the Ministry of Defence, the BBC and others, amounting to hundreds of millions of pounds. It came to public attention when serious problems arose in its healthcare division, which had contracts with the UK Department of Work and Pensions to set up and operate their system for determining fitness for work of some of the country's poorest and most vulnerable citizens.[17]

I don't mean to imply by these examples that such companies, or private business in general, are inherently incompetent or corrupt. But they clearly show that the private sector is not necessarily more competent or efficient than its public counterparts, and frequently much less so, even though this is given as one of the principal justifications for outsourcing and privatisation.

In 1992 the Conservative government of Prime Minister John Major launched its controversial 'Private Finance Initiative' (PFI), a form of public–private partnership that would allow governments in the UK to enter into often complex financial arrangements with private businesses for long-term public projects. The government's main motive here was less to carry on Margaret Thatcher's neoliberal crusade than to improve Britain's public accounts so it could meet the EU's Maastricht Convergence Criteria.

Initially, these projects were funded by the sale of bonds or with private bank loans which were repaid by the businesses involved from government funds during the lifespan of the contract. Not surprisingly, these proved to be attractive, low-risk deals for the companies, since governments rarely default. By 2007 the total capital value of PFI contracts signed throughout the UK was an extraordinary £68 billion, committing the British taxpayer to future spending of £215 billion for the duration of the long-term contracts. Then the financial crisis of 2008 struck and private capital dried up. So the government had to fund its 'private' finance scheme with public money, a situation eventually too absurd even for the Conservatives, although apparently not for Labour, which continued awarding PFI contracts using public money while it remained in power. The UK government finally announced in 2018 that it would no longer use PFI, though existing projects would continue to operate for some years to come.

It is little wonder that the British public has lost confidence in such 'market alternatives' to public services. A 2014 poll found that two-thirds do not trust private companies to deliver such services, and a 2018 Ipsos MORI poll showed that 33 per cent believe private businesses should play no role at all, up from 25 per cent in 2001.[18]

As mentioned, there has been very little privatisation in the US because public ownership there was rare to start with, but outsourcing by governments is now very extensive. According to a report by the US Congressional Research Service, there were 4,253,133 people working for the US Federal public service in 2020 (including military and postal workers).[19] This is nowhere near the number of people employed by private contractors, which is 12.7 million.[20]

The US military outsources an increasing amount of its work to private military companies (PMCs) or private security companies (PSCs), traditionally known as mercenaries. The American government (among others) made extensive use of them to support its operations in Iraq and Afghanistan in particular. These businesses are mainly staffed by ex-military and police and offer a range of 'services' to govern-ments, from advice and training to 'operational support' in combat zones. They are, by their nature, inherently secretive, so it is very difficult to determine what this industry is now worth, but one estimate values it at over $100 billion annu-ally, most of that public money.[21]

Free-for-All

The widespread deregulation of private industry and finance by governments all over the world beginning in the 1970s has been even more ruinous than privatisation and outsourcing have been. It culminated in the financial crisis of 2008, showing yet again that professional and ethical standards in private, profit-driven markets will slide inexorably to a dangerous and indecent level without vigorous state regulation. Yet govern-ments around the world lost sight of this truth when they crowded on to the deregulation bandwagon in the 1980s and 1990s.

The global economy was hit by a succession of shocks in the early 1970s, forcing politicians to question the standard assump-tions of postwar monetary and fiscal policy to deal with them. Petroleum shortages, rising unemployment and high inflation combined to create a political and intellectual environment in the West receptive to new ideas about the relationship between states and markets. The neoliberal view holds that, by removing obstacles to private capital through deregulation, privatising public enterprises and cutting corporation tax, the inherent efficiency and creativity of free markets can be maximised, thereby stimulating economic growth, technological innovation and general prosperity. Relentless and well-funded lobbying by business and pro-market think-tanks added to the pressure on lawmakers to deregulate private industry. The stage was set for the great neoliberal experiment to begin.

In the US transportation was the first major industry to be gradually deregulated, beginning with railroads in the wake of the 1970 collapse of Penn Central Transportation Company, the largest bankruptcy in US history to that point. In 1978 the US Congress passed the Airline Deregulation Act, which completely abolished the federal Civil Aeronautics Board, set up in 1938 to regulate all domestic interstate air transport. Laws deregulating buses, ocean transportation and freight soon followed. The trend then moved to energy, communications and finance. In most of these areas the changes produced unexpected and perverse effects that confounded the naïve expectations of their proponents, whose faith in the self-correcting efficiency of markets was a matter of theological certainty. The steady erosion of the Glass–Steagall reforms passed in the aftermath of the Great Depression, legally separating commercial and investment banking, unleashed a torrent of hype, reckless speculation and short-term profit-taking that came to define the 1990s. Its final demise in 1999 was cheered by Larry Summers, Bill Clinton's Secretary of the Treasury, who had lobbied for it. We may not all be Friedmanites, but Summers certainly was.

What formal regulation remained in place was often ineffective, sometimes deliberately so. Ever keen to maintain 'competitiveness' and appear 'business friendly' to potential investors and donors, politicians and civil servants often pressured regulatory agencies to apply the rules with a 'light touch', which helps to explain why they comprehensively failed to prevent the financial crisis of 2008. The regulators were usually hopelessly understaffed and underfunded, and suffered extensive 'regulatory capture', often developing a cosy client–patron relationship with the very industries they were meant to be policing. Often their staff left these hard-pressed government positions for more lucrative jobs in the companies that they had just been regulating, taking valuable knowledge with them. In the endless game of measure and countermeasure, the private mega-corporations played Goliath to the regulators' David, although rarely with the same satisfying biblical resolution.

This situation enabled Bernie Madoff to run the world's biggest Ponzi scheme for at least fifteen years right under the noses of the hapless Securities and Exchange Commission until his fraud imploded, despite frequent warnings that he was up to no good. The SEC also approved the 'mark-to-market' accounting method used by the energy firm Enron in its trading of natural gas futures contracts, the first non-financial company to do so. Enron abused this power to invent fanciful estimates of its own to mislead investors about the 'fair value' of the company, which was by then basically worthless. Enron's accounting firm, Arthur Andersen, also approved the mark-to-market accounting before it surrendered its licences to practise and declared bankruptcy.

According to the logic of neoliberalism, deregulation is setting markets free and, thereby, unleashing their inherent innovative and entrepreneurial potential. Only then can the marketplace do its 'magic'. Many governments, on both the left and the right, have been bewitched by such magical thinking. With few exceptions Western states in the 1980s began slashing regulations in the expectation economic miracles would follow. The labour market, finance, energy, oil and gas, electricity and transportation all experienced it. And reluctant governments in the developing world usually had deregulation forced on them by the IMF or the World Bank as one of the 'governance conditionalities' of the loans they received.

British governments have deregulated industries with religious zeal. One example must suffice: the 1986 Building Societies Act eroded the distinction between these traditional institutions and retail banks. Building societies are mutual companies (known as savings and loans societies in the US), owned by their members to provide them with services, in this case mortgages. There were once hundreds of them across

Britain. Their owners were typically workers and customers rather than shareholders, with a direct financial interest in the company. The 1986 Act allowed the societies to offer a range of financial services that had previously been restricted to banks. It also permitted them to demutualise and become public limited companies. A wave of demutualisations followed and most of Britain's building societies, some of which had been established in the eighteenth and nineteenth centuries, were converted into regular retail banks owned by shareholders, thereby breaking the mutuality that was their original basis.

Despite all this deregulation and 'light touch' enforcement, many medium and large businesses have still moved their corporate headquarters to overseas tax havens, not only to avoid taxes, but also to escape regulatory oversight in remote jurisdictions like the British Virgin Islands and Panama (among very many others) known not to ask too many awkward questions. They simultaneously evade national regulation of their businesses and weaken the ability of governments to provide essential goods and services by robbing them of tax and thereby imposing extra costs on the rest of society while still expecting the government to provide them with subsidies, free access to public infrastructure, and global military and legal protection for their assets.

The cycle of deregulation and reregulation is evidence that regulation is not enough. As soon as new regulations are enacted businesses start looking for ways to get around them and fund lobbying to rescind or weaken them. The only way to break this destructive cycle is through direct public ownership, as I will argue below.

Privatisation, outsourcing and deregulation are part of a revolutionary movement to fundamentally change the relationship between state and market by expanding the latter and contracting the former. It is based on ideal types of both derived from theoretical abstractions and ideological convictions rather than much direct experience of how either operate in the real world. Markets are naïvely assumed to be efficient, innovative and fair, since they are based on free transactions in a competitive environment where businesses always face the ultimate price for failure (bankruptcy), and states are naïvely assumed to be wasteful, coercive and incompetent, insulated from the consequences of their actions by taxpayer bailouts. Both assumptions are very misleading and partly account for the comprehensive failure of neoliberalism as an approach to governance and economics. I say 'partly' because there are no doubt many people (perhaps most) who actually work on the commanding heights of business who know perfectly well that these are just myths, albeit very profitable myths for them personally. It is impossible that such people don't know what is going on around them and have taken no advantage of that knowledge to enrich themselves even more.

Economically, this experiment has been an abject failure for all but a privileged few and has seriously damaged the lives of many. Politically, it has harmed most citizens by expanding the sphere of unaccountable private power over their lives, which now includes health, welfare, education and security. And it has diminished the ability of democratic governments to promote the public good and shape economic life in the interests of the majority to whom they are meant to be answerable. Neoliberalism represents more than just another failed policy. Privatisation in particular, and neoliberalism generally, presents us with a new understanding of the state and our role as citizens within it that is as radically different from what preceded it as the welfare state was to the classical state of the nineteenth century.

3

THE RISE OF PRIVATE GOVERNMENTS

On 4 August 2018, Apple became the world's first trillion-dollar company. Just two years later, it was worth two trillion dollars, more than the GDP of all but the seven wealthiest countries in the world. Amazon, Microsoft and Alphabet/Google have since followed Apple into the trillion-dollar club. Walmart, the world's largest retailer with global resources of nearly half a trillion dollars a year, is larger than two-thirds of the world's countries by annual GDP.[1] Two decades ago twenty-nine corporations were among the world's hundred largest economies; today there are forty-seven. Soon it will be over half.

The portion of the world's economy owned and controlled by the largest private corporations has increased dramatically in recent years, making them 'the dominant governance institutions on Earth'.[2] There has been a massive shift in the balance of wealth and power from states to markets over the last half-century, a process that has seriously undermined the power of national governments to promote the public good. It has also greatly enlarged the sphere of our lives that is dominated by private, secretive, unaccountable power.

Multinational corporations are nothing new; they have existed for centuries. The largest company in the world for nearly two centuries was the Dutch East India Company, established in 1602. It was one of a small number of international businesses at the time engaging in trade, exploration for and extraction of natural resources, and the promotion of European overseas settlement, each with a royal charter and a regional monopoly on trade.

The commercial corporation didn't become the dominant form of business organisation in the United States until its 'Gilded Age' in the late nineteenth century, a time of explosive industrialisation dominated by a small group of wealthy plutocrats such as John D. Rockefeller, Andrew Carnegie, J. P. Morgan and Cornelius Vanderbilt. These 'robber barons' built vast industrial empires in finance, oil and railroads, amassing unprecedented fortunes in the process. During this period of rapid industrial expansion the wealthiest 10 per cent of American households owned three-quarters of the nation's wealth,[3] while the bottom 40 per cent owned close to zero.[4] The new plutocrats of our own Gilded Age are multibillionaires Jeff Bezos, Bill Gates, Warren Buffett, Larry Ellison, Elon Musk and Mark Zuckerberg, the founders of the world's largest multinational businesses today, each with a personal fortune in the tens of billions of dollars. We are quickly regressing to the late nineteenth century.

These mega-corporations know the power they have and are not reticent about asserting it. Many are quite open about their aspiration for control, even though none of them is democratic or accountable to the populations they sell to. They have become informal private governments, exceeding most actual governments in wealth and power and increasingly beyond the reach of states to tax or regulate effectively. The balance of power in the world has shifted from traditional, territorially bound states to giant new leviathans of business that are dispersed across the globe in a world economy that increasingly ignores established political boundaries.

Corporate Leviathans

The earliest multinational corporations had charters directly from the Crown granting them a vast range of regional monopolistic powers, such as concluding treaties and alliances, maintaining armed forces, conquering territory and building forts. In return, the Crown took a share of their profits and could revoke its charters at will. Although private commercial ventures, these companies acted like private governments in the areas where they traded. The British East India Company had its own private army and navy to run the country until the British government took over direct rule of India in 1858. English colonies in North America were established by the London Company and the Plymouth Company, corporate entities that were granted royal charters by the king for the specific purpose of colonisation and conquest, just as the Hudson's Bay Company was chartered in 1670 to give this 'Company of Gentleman Adventurers' a monopoly of trade in what is now Canada. Yet these huge monopolistic charter companies were still subject to royal power to a much greater degree than today's multinational corporations are subject to state power.

There were very few of these charter companies at the time; since each one required royal permission, overseas travel, trade and exploration were extremely expensive and dangerous, and trade was severely limited by what was technologically possible in the seventeenth century. They operated from pre-industrial Europe, which was still overwhelmingly rural and followed mercantilist economic principles. Even by the end of the eighteenth century the new US Constitution made no mention of corporations, which barely existed in an economy still overwhelmingly dominated by agriculture, natural resources and small, family-owned farms and businesses. The first industrial revolution was just then beginning in Britain.

It wasn't until the second industrial revolution, which began in Britain around 1850, when it became possible to mass-produce steel cheaply, that large, heavy industries developed in the West and the number and size of corporations grew massively. Legal restrictions on the incorporation of businesses were eased at this time to facilitate industrial expansion. Companies went from being chartered by the Crown to being largely free of government direction. The first modern piece of company law was the British Joint Stock Companies Act (1844), which, for the first time in history, made it possible for ordinary people to incorporate a business through a simple process of registration rather than petitioning for a royal charter.

Britain's Limited Liability Act (1855) was transformative for capitalism since it allowed investors to limit their personal financial responsibility for business failure to the amount they had invested in them. This change 'made modern capitalism possible', according to the Cambridge economist Ha-Joon Chang, since it massively reduced the risk to individual investors.[5] It enabled the mobilisation of enormous sums of capital that were essential for the development of the newly emerging industries. Predictably, the number of companies in Britain soared in the wake of these crucial reforms. Countries across Western Europe and North America inevitably followed its example. Their economies were transformed from ones made up mainly of small workshops, family businesses and cottage industries to large manufacturing firms dominating entire industries. Many of these firms operated as cartels, rapaciously buying up their competitors or forcing them out of business.

By the late 1940s most of these international cartels that dominated the economies of the West were broken up as states forcefully reasserted themselves in economic life, particularly after the 1929 Wall Street crash. Multinational corporations lost much of their power and importance in the world economy to states during these decades. Many industries were nationalised by governments and the financial system was much more strictly regulated than in the past. We saw in Chapter One how many states embarked on an ambitious programme of nationalising industries such as steel, coal, gas, electricity, healthcare and railways. The main components of the welfare state were also constructed to increase access to public goods such as health and education for groups that had previously been excluded from them. Progressive income tax and corporation taxes rose steeply in these years to fund these developments and to redistribute wealth, leading to a decline in inequality. This was a period when the balance between state and market shifted dramatically back towards the former, so that 'national governments and labour unions provided effective countervailing power to the power of the private sector'.[6] A new consensus in favour of greater state involvement in the economy and a broad faith in the power of the state to promote the general welfare prevailed during this 'golden age of controlled capitalism'.[7]

In Chapter Two I outlined how, by the mid-1970s, the pendulum began to swing away from this statist consensus towards a new neoliberal 'Washington Consensus'. Increasingly, in elite circles, the state was seen as a threat to individual freedom and a hindrance to economic growth. According to the new 'Washington Consensus', the best prescription for the purported ills of the age is lowering taxes, reducing public spending, deregulating the economy, privatising state enterprises, liberalising international trade, and currency flotations. Deregulation of the banking system in particular led to a dramatic proliferation of offshore banks and facilitated capital flows across borders, eventually to the point that they could 'wash away all but the strongest governments'.[8] Technological advances in telecommunications and computing have also made it easier to collect, store and rapidly transmit information and capital around the world, further weakening national boundaries.

This was the beginning of the era of economic neoliberalism and the second rise of multinational corporations, whose relative importance in the world economy increased dramatically. In 1990 there were 35,000 multinational corporations in the world; by 2007 there were 79,000. While global GDP grew by 173 per cent from 1983 to 2001, the value of capital assets owned by the world's biggest corporations increased by 686 per cent over the same period.[9] The ratio of foreign direct investment (FDI) to gross domestic capital formation increased from 2 per cent around 1980 to 14 per cent in 1999; the ratio of the world's stock of FDI to world GDP increased from 5 to 15 per cent over the same period.[10]

The New Age of Oligopoly

This new age of multinational corporations is an age of oligopolies, in which a small number of very large sellers dominate in many key sectors of the economy. As the economies of the capitalist West have grown significantly, the number of firms within them has declined, leading to greater corporate concentration and reduced competition. In 1995 the top one hundred companies accounted for 53 per cent of all income from publicly traded firms and just 737 companies controlled 80 per cent of the total value of all transnational corporations in 2007.[11] By 2015 the top one hundred companies accounted for 84 per cent of all profits.[12] All of the world's major industrialised sectors are now controlled by, at most, five corporations, while 28 per cent have one corporation that accounts for more than 40 per cent of global sales.[13]

Google now has an almost 90 per cent market share as a search engine, and Facebook an almost 80 per cent share of social networks. Apple's iPhone and Google's Android completely control the mobile app market, and Amazon is by far the largest e-commerce seller, with an estimated market share of 43 per cent.[14] Today Boeing and Airbus between them have a 91 per cent share of the commercial aircraft manufacturing market. In the US about 60 per cent of automobile manufacturing is shared between four firms (Ford, Chrysler, General Motors and Toyota), and six firms (Disney, Time

Warner, CBS, Viacom, NBCUniversal and News Corporation) control 90 per cent of the mass media market. The music entertainment industry is dominated by Universal Music Group, Sony and Warner. In his book *The Myth of Capitalism*, Jonathan Tepper summarises what life is like for ordinary Americans in this system as follows:

> Late capitalism resembles Soviet logic when it comes to consumer options. When Americans wake up each day, they can get their cereal from Kellogg's, General Mills, or Post, who all together have an 85% share of the cereal market. At breaks from work, they might want a soft drink. The top three firms dominate more than 85% of the market. Coca Cola is the leader, followed by PepsiCo and Dr Pepper Snapple.[15]

Each passing decade seems to confirm Karl Marx's prediction that capitalism would become increasingly dominated by a smaller and smaller number of bigger and bigger firms, leading to an era of monopolies. Actually, we are now in a mixed era of monopoly and oligopoly capitalism. Marx foresaw that large firms would either buy up their smaller rivals or drive them out of business. Some companies have been known to cluster several of their shops in a small area just to force smaller local competitors out of business, even when doing so entails losses for them in the short term. Market leaders that are monopsonies – dominant buyers of certain products – can abuse this position to bully producers and suppliers, who have few alternatives they can sell to as the big supermarkets in the UK have long done to Britain's beleaguered dairy farmers. Sometimes dominant firms will agree among themselves to boycott a vendor in order to force him out of the market. Or a powerful firm may insist that weaker competitors boycott another competitor as a condition of doing business. Businesses are commonly fined for anticompetitive practices such as price-fixing, collusion, bid rigging, predatory pricing, tied selling and operating cartels. Often the fines are well below the value of the business that these corrupt practices earn, meaning they don't always act as a deterrent.

According to Marx, capitalists favour competition in theory but hate it in practice, since it tends to drive down profits. That is why he claimed that ideology inverts reality, so we don't perceive things as they really are, which would likely cause widespread outrage. It is usually the ideological partisans of capitalism, rather than its practitioners, who believe that capitalism is favourable to competition. Actual capitalists know better. The existence of antitrust laws and government regulatory agencies in all of the most economically active countries in the world shows just how strong the urge to dominate really is among these corporate behemoths. Wherever there are markets you will find laws and regulations designed to stop them from usurping competition. Yet all these laws and agencies have failed to prevent the development of capitalism into a system of oligopoly.

Perhaps most worrying of all now is the small number of tech giants that dominate the market. The ten richest companies in the world include Amazon, Facebook, Google, Apple and Microsoft, and their power is likely to continue growing. Some of these appear to have a disturbing reach that envelops most of the online public sphere and effectively allows them to control public communication, thereby threatening democratic politics. Accusations of censorship, shadow banning, de-monetising, algorithms, campaign funding and lobbying have been made against them and equally denied.

Unaccountable Power

The corporations that dominate the market today are not just getting larger in size and wealth and declining in number. They are also becoming increasingly global. Technological advances, particularly in transportation, communications and computing, have empowered companies to shift their production to those areas of the world where labour costs and taxes are low and regulations are light. This process has led to 'fine-slicing' by multinational corporations, where different aspects of their operations are split up into ever-narrower specialisations and dispersed across the globe to the locations optimally favourable to profit maximisation. A single 'corporate parent' can have hundreds, sometimes thousands, of subsidiaries spread around the world, each with a separate legal status that limits the liability of the parent.[16] Its corporate management will be in one country, financial assets in another, administrative staff dispersed across the globe, and factories producing goods wherever it is most cost-effective and expedient.

An army of expensive lawyers, accountants, bankers, agents, intermediaries and other professionals exist as enablers to set up and service this elaborate international system. Its true nature and extent were shockingly revealed in the so-called 'Panama Papers' in 2016. These leaked documents contained detailed personal financial information about many wealthy individuals and public officials that had previously been private. It was revealed that just one company had set up 214,000 shell companies to hide money for its rich clients. No one really knows how many of these have been set up by other firms but it is likely to add up to hundreds of thousands, if not millions.

This trend is apparent in the rapidly growing internationalisation of the legal profession. Law was traditionally restricted by national boundaries and lawyers were licensed to practise within them. However, with the globalisation of capitalism, increasing numbers of law firms have internationalised their practices to expand their opportunities for business. Global law firm networks have been built up, connecting thousands of professionals in dozens of countries. For example, one of the largest of these has over 21,000 lawyers in over 150 jurisdictions worldwide. With the global reach this provides it is better able to advise its wealthy clients on how to take maximum advantage of the increasingly global character of the market and the many opportunities it provides to evade taxes and regulations.

This global economic system has enabled the rich 'to live globally', in the words of Oliver Bullough, while 'the rest of us have borders' within which we are subject to laws and taxes.[17] Capitalism today has become substantially 'denationalised' and 'deterritorialised'. This vastly increases the available global supply of labour, which doubled between 1980 and 2000, 'expanding from around 1460 million workers to perhaps 3 billion in 2000'.[18] This has allowed firms to reduce their production costs and evade stricter regulation. It is now more difficult, bordering on impossible, for states to tax and regulate corporations. In fact, countries find themselves competing with each other to attract these corporations by offering lower taxes and less regulation. That is one reason corporate tax revenue as a proportion of total revenues has fallen in the US and has declined relative to the share of corporate profits in all of the OECD countries, further weakening the ability of states to provide services to their citizens and promote the public interest.

These increasingly stateless companies hide as much of their income as they can in tax havens, anonymous shell companies and offshore bank accounts. An estimated $32 trillion is parked offshore in tax havens, depriving governments of hundreds of billions of dollars in revenues worldwide, recently estimated in the region of $427 billion globally. While most multinational corporations are still nominally Western, the list of the five hundred largest industrial multinational corporations includes many more firms that are from outside the US and Europe. Today about one-third have their headquarters in Asia and Latin America.[19] And those that are still headquartered in the West now operate in ways that are increasingly international and complex, to maximise their position and profits.

The power of organised labour to constrain corporate power has diminished massively since the 1980s, when there was a large-scale shift in employment away from heavily unionised, high-wage sectors to more casual employment. Trade union membership was already in decline by then. At its peak in the mid-twentieth century, around a third of the American labour force was unionised. By 2012 it had fallen to just 11 per cent, roughly 5 per cent in the private sector and 40 per cent in the public sector. Trade union density has also declined sharply in many European countries, from 32.6 per cent in 1995 to 26.4 per cent in 2001 in the EU. Trade unions now represent a smaller proportion of the workforce in Europe than at any other time since 1950.[20] Not surprisingly, the effectiveness of strikes has declined sharply as companies after the 1970s could more easily close down factories and move them to low-wage countries with fewer health and safety regulations. The number of major work stoppages fell from 381 in 1970 to just eleven in

2010. Privatisation has transferred many jobs out of the public sector, where union membership is larger and more militant, to private firms, where fewer workers belong to unions. Today both governments and unions have much less power to check the behemoths of big business.

No multinational corporations are democracies, unlike many of the countries from which they have arisen. None are accountable to any general population, unlike democratic governments. So the shift in power from democratic states to multinational corporations has also necessarily reduced overall democratic accountability in the world. One aspect of neoliberalism is that less and less of our world is subject to the institutions of democratic governance. As the power of corporations over the lives of ordinary citizens steadily grows, people have less say in how they are governed by mammoth organisations managed by a wealthy elite that inhabits a rarefied world increasingly remote from the lives of those who buy the goods they produce and the services they sell.

Corporations are not only democratically unaccountable, they are also highly secretive. They are not open or transparent about their finances and operations to anything like the same degree as democratic governments, however far the latter fall short of complete openness. While most Western democracies conduct much of their business in public and are subject to freedom of information laws, albeit with many qualifications and loopholes, private corporations are not. Nor are enormously powerful international institutions like the World Trade Organization (WTO), the World Bank and the IMF, which conduct so much of their business behind closed doors. The men and women who run these powerful organisations are appointed, not elected, with little effective accountability to anyone.

In most jurisdictions private companies are not normally required by law to make most of their finances public. Most countries now require public companies to make some basic information about their directors, members, articles of association, annual accounts, company status and financial statements publicly available. In the UK, for example, the Companies Act (2006) requires corporate data relating to every limited company incorporated in the UK to be filed with the Companies House public register. However, there is no requirement to reveal any more information about company operations to the public and corporate tax returns are not normally made public.

It is now a widely acknowledged principle of good governance that the general public have a statutory right of access to data held by their government, with some restrictions. Today, over a hundred countries around the world have implemented some form of freedom of information legislation. This usually binds governments to promote openness and transparency, although the effectiveness of such laws is highly inconsistent and far from perfect. The UN's Sustainable Development Goal 16 has set targets to ensure public access to information and the protection of fundamental freedoms as a means to ensure accountable, inclusive and just institutions.[21]

Few of these laws include a similar right of access to private-sector data. As activities previously performed by governments are increasingly privatised and outsourced, this has reduced the scope of what is covered by freedom of information laws and transferred them to the more shadowy world of private corporations. These companies employ a wide range of complex legal and financial structures to hide their profits and business dealings from tax authorities, to launder money and to evade international economic sanctions. It also creates 'epistemic inequality' between governments and private companies, so the public can find out much more about the former than the latter. This often gives the misleading impression that governments are more prone to corruption and incompetence than corporations, which can more easily cover up such things.

Corporations exist to make profits, not to promote the public interest. The latter should be the responsibility of governments. The primacy of shareholder value has long been the key principle of corporate governance. Milton Friedman was strongly critical of managers who took anything into account in the operation of their business beyond strict profit maximisation. 'There is one and only one social responsibility of business', he wrote in 1962, 'to use its resources and engage in activities designed to increase its profits so long as it says within the rules of the game, which is to say, engages in open and free competition without deception or fraud.'[22] Like other market fundamentalists, Friedman believed that the public good is best served by each of us selfishly pursuing our own good in the competitive marketplace. Provided we each do this within the bounds of the law, there can be no conflict between the private interests of corporations and the public interest of citizens. Indeed, the public interest is just the sum of all these free transactions.

However, there has recently been a move by many of the world's multinational corporations, in principle if not in practice, away from traditional shareholder primacy towards a broader conception of corporate responsibility that includes all relevant stakeholders, such as consumers and shareholders. Many have joined the movement towards an 'inclusive capitalism' that is more socially progressive to improve their battered image after the financial crisis of 2008. The adoption of 'Corporate Social Responsibility' (CSR) is an attempt by CEOs and directors to change the culture and practices of their companies (or to appear to be doing so) in a way that broadens their goals and priorities without fundamentally altering capitalism. Eighty per cent of Davos business leaders now claim to reject the premise that a business's sole obligation is to increase share value.[23] This was formally expressed in the updated and expanded 2019 Business Roundtable definition of the purpose of the corporation, which has been signed by nearly two hundred CEOs of very large corporations.

An example of this trend is the so-called 'B Corporation' – certification of 'social and environmental performance', a private, voluntary, non-profit scheme set up to certify that its members meet standards that 'balance purpose and profit'. There is no formal mechanism for enforcing this very vague and general policy. Directors and officers of certified B Corporations are permitted to consider and prioritise the social and environmental impact of their decisions, rather than focus exclusively on maximising financial returns for shareholders. For example, directors might spend more money offsetting the environmental impact of their investment decisions at the expense of profits, unlike a traditional corporation. As of January 2021, there are over 3,700 certified B Corporations across 150 industries in 74 countries.[24]

Only mild cynicism is needed to see this 'Ben & Jerry's-fication of big business', in the words of Joel Bakan, as an elaborate PR exercise to improve the poor public image of corporations.[25] That is the main conclusion of Bakan's study of *The New Corporation*, which argues that progressive, socially minded capitalism and CEO activism are only being pursued to the extent that they do not fundamentally challenge the power and profits of corporations. They do not typically call for basic structural changes to the global economy or the adoption of macroeconomic policies that would very substantially improve the lives of the least well off. 'Though loudly proclaiming commitments to such values,' Bakan writes, 'they always limit their actions to measures that promote, or at least don't threaten, profitable practices and basic business models.'[26] Also, formally adopting a voluntary ethical code like this allows corporations to claim they are self-regulating and therefore don't need to be regulated by governments, something they are very keen to avoid.

More than eighty companies and CEOs issued statements of solidarity with Black Lives Matter in response to the murder of George Floyd in 2020.[27] And campaign donations by hedge funds, big tech companies and Fortune 500 firms overwhelmingly favoured Hillary Clinton and Joe Biden over Donald Trump in the 2016 and 2020 US presidential elections. Yet these same corporations spend millions every year lobbying politicians to cut taxes, reduce regulations and pass laws favourable to their narrow interests. In 2018 Facebook and Amazon each spent over $16 million on lobbying in Washington alone. Google spent almost $12 million.[28] Corporations like Coca-Cola, General Electric and IBM successfully lobbied governments for corporate tax cuts, 'securing new exemptions that reduced to almost nothing their tax liabilities for offshore profits, saving them tens of billions of dollars and allowing some of them, like Google, to abandon elaborate offshore tax-avoidance schemes'.[29]

Lately, many on both the left and the right have been preoccupied fighting culture wars, much to the delight of corporations, some of which have even joined in. Occupy Wall Street, which focused its anger on big business, has been replaced by Antifa, which is fighting fascism instead, sometimes in alliance with big business. No wonder corporate executives are now so keen to write cheques to support these causes. They provide them with a welcome distraction from debate about an economic system that benefits few people of any race or creed.

It is very naïve to think that corporations would ever voluntarily subordinate their own business interests to any cause that significantly undermined it, since profit is their *raison d'être*. At best, 'inclusive capitalism' is a mostly symbolic nod in the direction of greater social responsibility with little real substance, an elaborate but ultimately hollow form of corporate virtue signalling. At worst, it is a cynical rebranding exercise by savvy corporations to improve their public image and distract from their business-as-usual pursuit of power and profit.

Most countries in the world today are democracies in some minimal sense; very minimal in many cases. The Pew Research Center classifies 57 per cent of nations with populations of 500,000 or more as democratic 'in some form', up from just 24 per cent in 1977.[30] While too much can be made of these figures given that the meaning of 'democracy' is essentially contested, they are impressive compared to corporations. As of today no corporations are democracies, and there are many more corporations in the world than states. Some businesses in Germany, Austria and the Netherlands have a two-tiered board of directors, one of which (the executive board) runs its daily operations and the other (the supervisory board) represents shareholders and workers and determines who sits on the executive board and how they are compensated. But these are exceptions and fall short of full workplace democracy. In general, private corporations are run as autocracies with virtually no genuine accountability.

Like most autocracies, private corporations are instinctively secretive, particularly compared to democratic governments today, despite the lip service increasingly paid by businesses to 'transparency', 'accountability' and 'corporate responsibility'. This is partly because they are in direct competition with each other and therefore do not want all of their operations and finances disclosed. But that kind of reasonable argument for privacy is often used to shield the darker side of corporate activity, such as laundering hundreds of millions of dollars in drug proceeds for cartels, as HSBC did for a decade.[31] That is an extreme case, but corporate involvement in unethical and sometimes illegal activities is anything but rare. It is also increasingly difficult to detect. The obscurity in which much business is conducted today is not always intentional. Large multinational corporations are highly complex structures, often with thousands of subsidiaries dispersed over the planet in dozens of jurisdictions and employing hundreds of thousands of staff. But many of these firms deliberately do not disclose their sales, taxes or financial data from their foreign operations for reasons that have more to do with protecting their profits and institutional reputation than from any great respect for privacy. Sometimes the mask falls off, as it did in 2016 with the leaked 'Panama Papers', and we then catch a glimpse of some very ugly truths.

Governments are not wholly transparent either and democratic accountability is sometimes little more than a sham. However, in democratic states governments are ultimately answerable to the voters, unlike corporations, who are answerable only to their typically undemanding shareholders. And corporations always pursue one overriding goal – profit – which is their reason for existing. No states are indifferent to wealth and power, even democracies, but few are entirely indifferent to the public good either, if only because it is risky to ignore it completely. It is no concern of business though.

4

PREYING ON THE WEAK

The assassination of Édgar Millán Gómez in his own home in 2008 was shocking evidence of both the power of Mexico's drug cartels and the limitations of the Mexican state that was at war with them. Millán Gómez was the national coordinator of his country's fight against organised crime, the nation's third-ranking police official and acting commissioner of the elite Federal Preventive Police. He was also the third leading Mexican security official to be killed in a week. Just days before, Roberto Velasco Bravo, director of a federal organised-crime unit, and José Aristeo Gómez, chief of staff of the Federal Preventive Police in Mexico City, were murdered by the drug cartels.[1]

That some of the most senior commanders of the country's police could be murdered in a single week was a brazen challenge to the authority of the Mexican state. Politicians, journalists, judges and police are all now regularly killed by the drug cartels, who operate as paramilitary organisations using military-style tactics. All of them employ thousands of men armed with heavy-calibre machine guns, high explosives, rocket-propelled grenades, guided missiles, surveillance equipment, ships, light aircraft and even submarines. Most were trained either in paramilitary camps run by the cartels themselves or by the Mexican Army. After training many cartel members had deserted the military for the more lucrative prospects of the illicit drug trade. By 2010 there were twelve thousand drug-related murders in Mexico in one year, up from just a thousand in 2001.[2] This figure would continue to climb, particularly after 2015. On average there were around thirty thousand homicides per year in Mexico during the presidency of Enrique Peña Nieto. When he left office at the end of 2018, the figure was over 33,000, the highest on record to that point. Between one-third and one-half of these murders were likely the result of organised crime. It is estimated that such deaths globally now far exceed the number of casualties caused by armed conflict and terrorism.[3] By the twenty-first century Mexico's drug cartels had become the 'biggest armed threat to Mexico since its 1910 revolution', according to Ioan Grillo, author of *El Narco* (2012) about the cartels.[4]

Criminal organisations operate in every country in the world and always have. They are nothing new. And all criminality is a formal challenge to the state's authority because it involves the violation of its laws. Strong states, which are typically also rich states, are usually equipped to meet such challenges, although they sometimes cede authority to criminals in exceptional circumstances. Even an otherwise strong state like Mexico has pockets of fragility, as its drugs war has revealed. The Italian Mafia has assassinated many state officials, such as judges, prosecutors, senior police officers and politicians, particularly during the 1980s. Among the most prominent and audacious of these was the murder of General Carlo Alberto dalla Chiesa in 1982. He had been serving as prefect for Palermo in Sicily, working to end the Second Mafia War there, when he and his wife were shot by mafiosos. Two years later the Mafia exploded a bomb on an express train between Naples and Milan, killing sixteen and wounding 266. Another Mafia terrorist campaign in the early 1990s targeted popular tourist destinations in Milan, Florence and Rome, killing ten.

But fragile states, which are typically also poor states, are much more vulnerable than comparatively strong and wealthy states like Mexico and Italy. Because of their weakness they are often forced into a range of different relations with criminal organisations, some confrontational and others collaborative. At one extreme, such states fight protracted wars against criminal insurgents and, at the other extreme, they enter into mutually beneficial strategic alliances with organised crime.

The end of the Cold War and the advance of globalisation have increased the opportunities for organised criminality. The serious weakening of some states caused by major political upheavals such as the collapse of communism and the increasing movement of people, money and goods across borders have opened up spaces for criminals to operate, which is why more attention is now paid to transnational criminal organisations (TCOs) than in the past, when criminality was more localised and borders less permeable. While they almost never seek to overthrow states per se, many of these groups aim to reduce state power in some spheres, even to the point of taking control over territory within them or sharing authority with the state.

Fragile states are also very vulnerable to the power of the international agencies that now dominate the global economic system. These include the World Trade Organization, the World Bank and the International Monetary Fund, among others. Such states tend to be 'rule takers' in our global economic system, rather than 'rule givers', which consist mainly of rich states and the international agencies they fund. While such agencies don't use armed force, unlike criminal groups, they wield vast economic power that can be more damaging to the authority of the states who are subject to it than physical force. Weak states are often squeezed between well-armed criminal organisations within and dictatorial economic institutions without. Both show little mercy towards states that are usually too weak to fight back in countries with some of the poorest and most desperate people in the world.

Mafia Capitalism

The Institutional Revolutionary Party (PRI) held power in Mexico continuously from 1929 until 2000. Even when Vincente Fox won the 2000 presidential election against the PRI, it still held most of the state governments. It is no coincidence that the seven decades of PRI government in Mexico were an era of relatively low violence compared to the two decades since. In fact, homicides declined there until the twenty-first century, when they shot up faster than almost any other country in the Western hemisphere. During its seventy-one-year reign, the PRI was able to manage and contain criminal violence, often by means of corruption and collaboration with organised crime.

Colombia, by contrast, struggled for decades to defeat various paramilitary groups, guerrilla insurgencies and criminal syndicates that have fought the government for control. The country's powerful drug cartels were active participants in this very bloody conflict, most notoriously the Medellín cartel run by Pablo Escobar, the 'King of Cocaine'. He is believed to have ordered the assassination of Colombia's minister of justice Rodrigo Lara and the presidential candidate Luis Carlos Galán, who supported Escobar's extradition to the United States.

Escobar even backed the attack on the Colombian Supreme Court by M-19 guerrillas in 1985 because it was then considering the constitutionality of the country's extradition treaty with the US. Such direct defiance of the state is extreme even by the standards of the region, with its long history of revolutions, insurgencies and organised criminality.

When the US successfully shut down the smuggling of Colombian cocaine into the US via the Caribbean, Colombia's cartels partnered with their Mexican counterparts to supply the vast and insatiable American drug market, estimated to be worth over US$60 billion a year, by alternative routes across the US–Mexican border. By the time Escobar was finally killed in 1993, power had already begun to shift to the Mexican cartels, who now control much of the drug supply chain into the United States. They are also involved in a huge range of crimes beyond drugs, including extorting money from bars and discos, demanding 'protection' money from businesses, taking money from prostitution rings and human trafficking, car theft, and stealing crude oil and gasoline.

One of the most violent Mexican drug syndicates is Los Zetas, notorious for their terroristic tactics, including beheadings, torture, car bombings and random violence, which were later adopted by other criminal groups in the region. As their power grew the Zetas acted more like a paramilitary insurgency than a conventional criminal gang. They took on the government directly, launching audacious attacks on the police and military and fighting pitched battles with them. 'Their revolt against civil authority', writes Ioan Grillo, 'includes attacks by more than fifty men on army barracks; assassination of high-ranking police and politicians; and mass kidnappings of ten or more policemen and soldiers.'[5]

In addition to fighting the Mexican state, the Zetas battled the rival Sinaloa Cartel led by Joaquín Archivaldo Guzmán Loera, popularly known as 'El Chapo'. When the Mexican Federal Police arrested Guzmán in 2016 he was one of the richest and most powerful drug lords in the country. Before his arrest *Forbes* magazine included him on its list of the world's billionaires, alongside Warren Buffett, Jeff Bezos and Bill Gates.[6]

Together, the Mexican drug cartels take in between $19 billion and $29 billion annually from drug sales in the US.[7] The Sinaloa Cartel's slice of this huge criminal cake is around $4.75 billion annually, although most of it is not profit, owing to the high costs of running an operation like drug trafficking. And the Mexican drug cartels are only part of the global narco-economy, which is estimated to be worth between US$426 billion and US $652 billion annually, according to the 2017 Global Financial Integrity report on 'Transnational Crime and the Developing World'. The report estimates the total revenues generated by the eleven major categories of crime it covers to be between US$1.6 trillion and US$2.2 trillion annually.[8] According to Ioan Grillo, the illegal drug trade helped to keep the Mexican peso afloat during the financial crisis of 2008. 'It rivals Mexico's big sources of foreign currency,' he writes. 'In 2009, oil exports were worth $36.1 billion; remittances sent home from Mexican migrants were $21.1 billion; and foreign tourism brought in $11.3 billion. Drug money would be number two on that list.'[9] Drug cartels today are comparable in size, complexity and wealth to large multinational corporations, generating billions of dollars annually. This partly explains the viciousness of the fighting between the cartels and the government, given how much is at stake.

Mexico's huge drug cartels benefit from their proximity, on one side, to the vast US drugs market and, on the other side, to countries like Colombia, Peru and Bolivia that are major suppliers of heroin. But illegal drugs are trafficked all over the world. The so-called 'Golden Triangle' in Southeast Asia, where the borders of Thailand, Laos and Myanmar meet, is a major hub of the global drug trade. Opium and heroin are grown in the region then transported to labs to be refined into heroin for sale around the world. Synthetic drugs – amphetamines, methamphetamine and ecstasy, as well as synthetic versions of cannabis and of opioids such as heroin – are also mass-produced in the region. Much of this system is controlled by Chinese triads, which have bases throughout the Golden Triangle and far beyond it. Sam Gor, also known as 'The Company', is the name of an organised criminal syndicate consisting of several different triads headed by the Chinese-Canadian Tse Chi Lop,

Asia's 'El Chapo', until his arrest in 2021. Sam Gor lies at the centre of the Asian drug trade worth an estimated $70 billion a year. According to the UN Office on Drugs and Crime, Sam Gor alone is responsible for between $8 billion and $17.7 billion of this.[10]

Although Mexico's cartels have not come anywhere close to toppling the federal government in the country's drug war, they have been successful in establishing operational control in many local areas through mass intimidation and bribery. A 2010 study commissioned by the Mexican Senate found that 195 municipalities (8 per cent of the total) were 'completely under control of organised crime' and another 1,536 (63 per cent of the total) reportedly were 'infiltrated' by organised crime.[11] They also exert considerable influence on the federal government and law enforcement by buying off politicians and officials, including at the very highest levels of state. Even in a relatively strong state like Italy, organised crime has corrupted politics at every level. The former Italian prime minister Giulio Andreotti was prosecuted for allegedly colluding with the Mafia, although he was acquitted. Hundreds of local councils in Italy have been dissolved by the police for having ties with organised crime.

Criminal organisations often provide basic public services to locals and even some measure of governance in situations where they have a degree of effective control. By competing with the state in the provision of such services, they usurp its role and undermine its legitimacy with the local population, particularly if they do a better job than the government. In many cases criminals will 'tax' businesses for these services, including providing 'protection', thereby further weakening the state, which may be unable to extract its own taxes in such situations.

Organised criminal networks do not always directly challenge the laws and authority of the states they operate within. Their relationship is far more complex than mere opposition. They also collaborate with them for their mutual benefit. For example, the military and police may form a tactical alliance with one drug cartel to better eliminate or weaken another. The Guatemalan military sometimes used this method in the country's long civil war. Several African countries have been known to 'outsource' the use of force to mercenaries and criminal groups, and the government of Yugoslavia relied on paramilitary groups to help fight its opponents. Criminal organisations may also bribe public officials and members of the military to turn a blind eye to their activities or even to support them. At one point in the 1990s it was found that thirty-four high-ranking public security officials, including the head of the federal anti-drug agency, had been working for organised crime in Mexico.[12] In 2008 Operation Clean House in that country uncovered a network of twenty-five federal officials on the payroll of the Sinaloa Cartel, including soldiers, federal police commanders and detectives. In extreme cases, the state, or parts of it, may be captured by criminal networks, blurring the distinction between legitimate government and organised crime. This is more likely in fragile states that lack the resources to compete with powerful criminal rivals, or in countries suffering economic and political turmoil. Russia after the fall of communism may be an example of this situation, as well as various 'narco-states' such as Bolivia, Nigeria, Ghana and Guinea-Bissau.

The Russian state was severely weakened after 1990, which created an irresistible opportunity for criminal networks there to expand and thrive. By the turn of the century there were thousands of them, including several large, well-organised and heavily armed mafia groups, the 'vory' (thieves) as they are known, with extensive international connections. Russia during these years was a 'gangster's paradise', as Mark Galeotti, a leading authority on the subject, has described it, operating a system of 'mafia capitalism'.[13] Many ex-soldiers, including veterans of the Afghanistan war, were in big demand by criminal organisations that relied heavily on force and coercion. But as the Russian state has reasserted itself under Vladimir Putin, the mafia has become less wild and overtly violent, more subtle and sophisticated. As Galeotti writes:

the modern Russian state is a much stronger force than it was in the 1990s, and jealous of its political authority. The gangs that prosper in modern Russia tend to do so by working with rather than against the state. In other words:

do well by the Kremlin, and the Kremlin will turn a blind eye. If not, you will be reminded that the state is the biggest gang in town.[14]

Even a society as orderly and crime-free as Japan, with a very strong state, has a well-established and active organised crime network (the 'Yakuza'), which is tolerated partly because it is no threat to the state and rarely engages in violence against it, unlike the Latin American drug cartels and the Italian Mafia. With around 25,000 active members, a mere fraction of its peak in the 1960s, it is still a substantial criminal presence in a nation where levels of criminality are extremely low compared to other industrial societies. Organised crime exists to some degree in all states, even the strongest and most stable, and therefore drains their resources and undermines their laws. But it only poses a real threat to few states and, even there, usually only to some parts of them.

Organised crime naturally thrives on the open oceans, outside of the boundaries of states, in the form of seaborne piracy, which is estimated to cost $16 billion a year in losses. Hotspots are regions with high concentrations of commercial shipping, such as the waters between the Red Sea and Indian Ocean, off the Somali coast, the Strait of Malacca and Singapore. Narrow waters such as the Gulf of Aden are particularly dangerous for cargo ships because small, fast motorboats are more likely to find and overtake them there.

Also, they may need to reduce their speed in coastal waters for navigation and safety reasons, making them easier prey for raiders. Offshore oil and gas production installations have also been targets of pirates. Shipping companies now regularly employ private armed security on their ships and facilities to deter attacks. These attacks usually occur outside the boundaries of states and are not (yet) on a scale comparable to organised crime within states.

The opportunities for hiding wealth for criminal purposes and tax avoidance have grown dramatically with the proliferation of offshore banking, complex money-laundering schemes, cryptocurrencies and wire transfers. Only seventy-five banks were offshore tax havens in 1979, where now there are thousands. A trillion dollars are sent by international money transfers annually.[15] Many Russian oligarchs who benefited from the economic chaos of the Yeltsin years moved their wealth out of the country as soon as they could. Joseph Stiglitz, who was chief economist of the World Bank from 1997 to 2000, writes that the 'IMF had lent Russia the dollars – funds that allowed Russia, in turn, to give its oligarchs the dollars to take out of the country. Some of us quipped that the IMF would have made life easier all around if it had simply sent money directly into the Swiss and Cyprus bank accounts.'[16] In that case, the weakness of the post-Soviet state facilitated such theft, which robbed the Russian government of revenue that further weakened it, creating a vicious circle. The global 'tax gap' caused by tax evasion and avoidance is estimated to be around half a trillion dollars. Sometimes the state itself is criminal, with public officials appropriating funds for their own use, thereby undermining it from within and corroding trust in government.

Cryptocurrencies are increasingly popular with people looking to avoid the law because they are anonymous. The most popular of these is Bitcoin, which is a decentralised digital currency launched in 2009. Its transactions are encrypted so that they are beyond the reach of either governments or banks, involving peer-to-peer exchanges that bypass intermediaries. This is ideal for use in dark web marketplaces, where illicit goods and services can be bought anonymously. Like Bitcoin, the dark web uses complex, layered encryption and inter-mediate servers that prevent its users' locations or identity from being traced. Accessing the dark web and its special browsers also requires custom software. Obviously all kinds of crimi-nality flourishes within this murky, anonymous world, such as posting and accessing child pornography and violent images, the sale and purchase of illegal goods like drugs and weapons, cyber extortion, money laundering, fraud, scams, hacking and collecting funds for terrorism. However, given its nature, it is impossible to confirm how much, if any, of this actually goes on and, if so, on what scale. So, while cryptocurrencies and the dark web are designed to bypass states and their legal systems, it is unclear how much of a threat they really pose.

Faustian Pacts

During the 1980s debt crisis in Latin America, commonly referred to there as 'the lost decade', a cartoon appeared in a Mexican newspaper showing an ordinary worker hanging from a scaffold. A well-dressed man is taking the last of the dying worker's money from his pockets. On his briefcase are the letters 'IMF'.

Between 1970 and 1980, Latin America's debt levels skyrocketed by more than 1,000 per cent. By the early 1980s, many countries in the region were struggling to pay the interest on this money, let alone the principal. In August 1982 this ticking debt time-bomb exploded when Mexico's government announced that it was no longer able to service its public debt of $85 billion. Many other countries in the region were in the same dilemma or close behind. Predictably, private banks immediately stopped lending to them and tried to call in their outstanding loans. This plunged these countries even deeper into crisis.

The US government and the International Monetary Fund intervened to contain the spiralling problem. The IMF agreed to act as 'international lender of last resort' to the struggling governments of Latin America, comparable to a loan shark. It would loan them funds to pay the interest on their debt in return for agreeing to sweeping 'structural reforms' to their domestic economies. Much of this money loaned by the IMF ended up back in Wall Street as these beleaguered nations used it to pay the interest on their original loans from American banks. The power of the IMF increased to unprecedented levels over these countries, who had no other source of foreign capital. They were forced to implement deep cuts to spending on infrastructure, health and education, causing enormous suffering to their populations. Public-sector pay was frozen or cut and many lost their jobs. Unemployment shot up (which increased spending on welfare and reduced tax revenues), growth plunged and living standards dropped sharply. The case of Brazil is typical:

> As a result of the IMF conditionality policies, Brazil experi-enced a four percent drop in its Gross Domestic Product (GDP), a 211 percent rise in inflation, and a twelve percent decline in employment by the end of 1983. Consequently, an economic recession arose which provoked urban food riots by the unemployed and impoverished. In 1984, Brazilians directed over 900 riots in Rio de Janeiro, Sao Paulo, and other urban centers against the IMF as the alleged source of their socioeconomic problems. Brazil's Gross Domestic Product declined from $296 billion in 1982 to only $226 billion in 1985. As of 1988, almost half of Brazil's population lived in households where income was less than one hundred and twenty dollars a month.[17]

Then, as now, the IMF was dominated by the rich developed countries of the West, especially the US. As we have already seen, the neoliberal revolution with its deep faith in 'the miracle of the marketplace' and strong scepticism about governments had already begun in the West. The IMF's policy prescriptions for Latin America were rooted in this faith and had little regard for either their devastating effects on ordinary people or the traditions of the region, where the state had played a large role in promoting development, for example through the operation of state enterprises or by directing capital towards favoured sectors. Suddenly imposing market-oriented policies on such countries as a condition of loans provoked a fierce and predictable backlash that explains the Mexican cartoon mentioned above and helped to condition the political changes that later occurred in South and Central America. Even though over $60 billion of the region's public debt to foreign private banks was later written off, the damage had been done by then. Little wonder Joseph Stiglitz has compared this approach to warfare: 'Modern high-tech warfare is designed to remove physical contact: dropping bombs from 50,000 feet ensures that one does not "feel" what one does. Modern economic management is similar: from one's luxury hotel, one can callously impose policies about which one would think twice if one knew the people whose lives one was destroying.'[18]

Greece suffered a similar fate in the wake of the global financial crisis of 2008. Between 2009 and 2017 its debt-to-GDP ratio shot up from 127 per cent to 179 per cent. A sovereign debt crisis led the Greek government to seek an emergency bailout from a 'Troika' of institutions: the European Central Bank (ECB), the European Commission and the IMF. The latter played a subordinate role in this case, partly because it actually favoured a more gradual policy than its even more hardline European partners, who were dominated by Germany. But the IMF went along in requiring the standard prescription of steep tax rises and massive cuts to public spending – the usual harsh medicine with the usual harsh results.

When these policies only deepened Greece's crisis, more bailouts became necessary, involving even greater austerity. Prior to the third bailout in 2015, the Greek government of Prime Minister Alexis Tsipras held a referendum asking his compatriots to vote on whether the country should accept more austerity as a condition of another bailout. Tsipras campaigned for a 'No' vote. 'I call on you to say a big "no" to ultimatums, "no" to blackmail,' he declared to his fellow citizens. 'Turn your back on those who would terrorise you.' The result was 61 per cent against. Yet Tsipras ignored the outcome of the referendum and reached a deal with the 'Troika' that imposed even harsher austerity than the Greeks had just rejected in their national vote. The Greek government would be required to increase corporate tax and VAT, cut public-sector pay even more, end early retirement and undertake another round of privatisations. A more flagrant disregard for democracy is hard to imagine. It shows the extent to which Greece is now effectively governed by foreign bankers and international bureaucrats.

The IMF is a key institution in the new system of global economic governance set up at the end of World War Two. Delegates from the Allied nations met for a UN Monetary and Financial Conference in Bretton Woods, New Hampshire in 1944 to create rules and institutions to regulate the international monetary system (the 'Bretton Woods System'). The agreement between the states that signed on established a new set of international institutions to oversee this system, headquartered in Washington DC. Today only a small number of countries like Cuba and North Korea are not IMF signatories. When member states get into serious financial difficulty, they can turn to the IMF for loans, usually as a last resort, as in the case of Mexico in 1982. This is a Faustian pact because it means accepting very strict conditions, which usually include major cuts in public spending, trade liberalisation, the removal of price controls and state subsidies, and rapid and extensive privatisations. Priority is given to keeping inflation down and budget deficits low, consistent with the monetarist assumptions of the 'Washington Consensus' rather than the IMF's original Keynesian approach, where governments played a key role in job creation through public spending to stimulate growth and employment. Instead, the IMF now forces the countries it bails out to accept a one-size-fits-all neoliberal approach that is based on the belief that only such bitter medicine will stimulate growth, create jobs, increase revenues, lower public expenditure and create a path from crisis to prosperity. The effect has usually been reduced growth, increased unemployment and cruel austerity for those who are most dependent on state support. Thailand was not bailed out in the late 1990s until it agreed to cut social spending in healthcare and education, which led to a surge in AIDS infections and prostitution. Fortunately, there are some signs that the IMF is now moving away from its neoliberal stance, which was so obviously counterproductive in Greece.[19]

The IMF is regularly and rightly criticised for its system of internal governance. By convention its managing director is from Europe and its deputy managing director from the US, something that is increasingly resented by the world's rising economic powers like Brazil and India. Rich Western countries are overrepresented on the Fund's twenty-four-member Executive Board. The United States, Japan, China, Germany, France, the United Kingdom and Saudi Arabia each get to appoint their own executive director to the Board. The remaining seventeen directors represent constituencies consisting of two to twenty-three countries. Voting at the IMF is based on a complex quota system that reflects each member's relative economic position in the world ('one-dollar-one-vote'). Any change in the voting shares requires approval by a super-majority of 85 per cent of voting power. The IMF's directors are appointed rather than elected and broadly reflect the distribution of wealth and power in the world today. Yet most of the countries they end up 'helping' are in the developing world, which has frequently led to accusations of neo-colonialism. The IMF typically deals directly with finance ministers and central bankers in recipient countries who are unrepresentative of the majority of people there. All of this secretive elite deal-making weakens the Fund's legitimacy in the eyes of many ordinary people who bear the brunt of its often harsh policies. And it raises serious questions about the IMF's accountability, particularly when it intrudes itself into the domestic politics of recipient countries, as it usually does.

The Bretton Woods Conference in 1944 also created the World Bank (WB), headquartered in Washington like the IMF. It consists of the International Bank for Reconstruction and Development (IBRD), the lending arm of the WB, and the International Development Bank (IDB), set up in 1958, as well as some smaller institutions. By convention the president of the WB Group is an American. The WB was established to provide cheap loans to developing countries for long-term projects that would strengthen their economies, reduce poverty and improve quality of life, particularly in areas such as health, education and transportation. Its remit is structural, whereas the IMF's is macroeconomic. The WB has the same basic internal governance structure as its cousin, and therefore the same basic problems of accountability and legitimacy as the IMF.

Like the IMF, the WB is a central component of the postwar global financial system that has shifted power away from states and towards elite international economic institutions, particularly in the developing world. Since these institutions are dominated by the most developed industrial states, which are themselves in thrall to the world's largest banks and corporations, they have greatly enhanced the power of the latter. The WB shares the same monetarist ideology as the IMF and uses economic leverage to force recipient countries into accepting it as a condition of the loans it grants them. This undermines the independence of these states and weakens their domestic political institutions, which are often sidelined by the agreements signed behind closed doors between the WB and national elites.

The other major institutional pillar of the global governance system is the World Trade Organization (WTO), which was set up in 1995 with headquarters in Geneva. It deals with disputes between its members based on the terms of the trade agreements that they all sign when they join. Its decisions are final and cannot be appealed. And its negotiations are conducted in secret, so it too lacks accountability and transparency, two of the basic principles of democracy. We cannot see what factors influence its deliberations or what pressures are applied to it and from what quarters, although it is easy enough to imagine. Its governing structure is more 'democratic' than its sister institutions, the IMF and the WB, because WTO members each have one vote, so poorer countries can outvote richer countries ('one-member-one-vote'). But in practice it is dominated by much the same global economic elite as the other institutions that now dominate world trade and finance. This can be seen in its policies, which often involve lowering trade barriers and tariffs, particularly in sectors where the wealthiest countries are strongest. Infant industries in less developed economies are often exposed to unfair competition from larger and more mature market competitors as a result. In such situations, a policy of import duties, tariffs, subsidies and quotas may be more appropriate to nurture sectors of the economy that would be overwhelmed by free trade. The series of protests that were held at the 1999 WTO Ministerial Conference in Seattle were a dramatic expression of the degree of popular anger at the power and policies of these unaccountable institutions and the system of global capitalism that they serve. It was dissatisfaction with these institutions that caused China to propose an alternative, the Asian Infrastructure Investment Bank (AIIB), which was officially launched in Beijing in 2014. Among its fifty-seven prospective founding members are all of the world's major economies except the US and Japan. It is likely that Japan will join eventually.

The philosopher Jean-Jacques Rousseau claimed that what is most necessary is that governments 'protect the poor against the tyranny of the rich'. Traditional tyrants usually came in the form of police and soldiers acting on the orders of a classic dictator like Stalin. But they can appear as tattooed gangsters acting as the agents of a psychopathic billionaire drug lord, or wearing a suit, carrying a briefcase and claiming 'we're here to help'. Between rapacious, homicidal drug gangs and zealous 'market Bolsheviks' from the IMF (to borrow Joseph Stiglitz's apt term for the latter), the poor of the developing world have been the easy prey of powers inside and outside the states they inhabit, particularly when their own governments have been complicit with both. In that case there's little they can do to protect them-selves. But states can and sometimes do protect their citizens from such predators. Countless agents of the state – brave soldiers, judges, police officers, prosecutors and politicians – have been killed fighting organised crime. Fewer have stood up to the bullying of the international agencies that are dominated by rich Western democracies, although there are signs of that changing now, particularly in South and Central America, which have suffered more than most from every kind of tyranny.

5

WISHFUL THINKING
BETWEEN STATE
AND MARKET

It began in Poland and soon spread across Eastern Europe and beyond. A massive wave of nationwide strikes began on 21 April 1988 and continued for four months until the Communist government, surprised and shaken by their scale, agreed to negotiate with Solidarity, the underground trade union movement headed by Lech Walesa, who led the successful strike. Legislative elections the following year gave Solidarity an overwhelming victory and resulted in the appointment of a coalition government with the country's first non-Communist prime minister in forty years. Walesa was elected president of Poland in 1990.

The collapse of four decades of Communist rule in Czechoslovakia followed a similar pattern. It began with a student demonstration in Prague in November 1989. The Communist regime's attempt to crush it transformed the demonstration into the 'Velvet Revolution' that brought half a million Czechs into the streets of the capital and led to a nationwide general strike. Ten days later the Communist Party ended its monopoly of power and handed the government over to non-communists. Czechoslovakia then held its first democratic elections in over four decades. Václav Havel's Civic Forum party won the largest number of seats and he became the country's president in 1993.

And so an irresistible chain reaction had begun that would lead, by the end of 1991, to the collapse of the Soviet Union, the dissolution of the Warsaw Pact and the election of Boris Yeltsin as president of the new Russian Federation. Communist ideology was abandoned with stunning rapidity by states beyond Europe as well. In the early 1990s many regimes across Africa and Asia ceased to be officially communist.

Meanwhile, as we saw in Chapter Two, governments in the West were also turning against the state as an obstacle to freedom and prosperity rather than as an agency for their promotion. Both the popular opposition to Communist rule in the East and the widespread abandonment of statist economic policies in the West in the immediate post-Cold War world were part of a general 'renaissance of civil society',[1] when hopes for the future shifted from the state to the sphere of voluntary, self-organising, non-governmental groups and associations that were credited with toppling autocratic regimes in the Eastern Bloc. It was a moment of soaring expectations about the popular democratic potential of autonomous, grassroots civil society groups to force political change on governments.

But such high hopes have not survived the reality of 'civil society' today, which is very rarely the space where free associational activity flourishes and popular power is expressed, as it was in Eastern Europe a generation ago. Then, there was no market to speak of in the Warsaw Pact countries. Today the sphere of 'civil society' has been thoroughly penetrated by market forces that are dominated by vast, predatory corporations and envelop us in an inescapable culture of consumerism and advertising. Whereas in the East it was the state that colonised civil society in the twentieth century, today it is the market that colonises it. Civil society survived twentieth-century communism, which failed to destroy it completely, but very little of it has survived twenty-first-century capitalism.

The term 'civil society' is broad and loose, which may explain why it has proponents across the ideological spectrum. It is a common criticism that it is inherently vague, perhaps to the point of meaninglessness. It is an umbrella concept that encompasses a wide range of private groups, institutions and networks outside of government. However it is defined, all agree that relations between citizens in 'civil society' are voluntary and are not mediated through the state, although some states fund some voluntary associations. In Canada, for example, many ethnic and cultural groups receive state funding as part of the official government policy of 'multiculturalism'. This blurs the line between state and civil society and inevitably raises questions about how independent such groups really are from the governments that fund them.

Relationships within 'civil society' are often described as 'horizontal', directly connecting freely associating individuals and groups, rather than 'vertical', as between citizens and the state or between patrons and their clients. There are two basic types of civil society groups: member-serving and public-service. The former exist to support the activities of people who have shared interests, such as sports clubs, choral societies, business and professional associations, and trade unions. The latter are altruistic voluntary organisations that promote humanitarian causes such as education, healthcare, social welfare, women's rights and animal welfare.

Little Platoons

In the 1830s, the French politician and writer Alexis de Tocqueville toured the United States to make a survey of its prisons and penitentiaries. He travelled widely and made extensive notes of his impressions of early American society, which he published as the enormously influential, two-volume *Democracy in America* (1835 and 1840). Tocqueville, a citizen of France with its strong, centralised state, was powerfully struck by the comparative weakness of American government and the great number and vibrancy of its voluntary civil associations. With a national government remote from their lives, individuals in 1830s America often took matters into their own hands rather than waiting for the state to step in and solve common problems, a situation so contrary to French experience. Tocqueville wrote admiringly:

> Americans of all ages, all conditions, and all dispositions, constantly form associations. . . . The Americans make associations to give entertainments, to found seminaries, to build inns, to construct churches, to diffuse books, to send missionaries to the antipodes; they found hospitals in this manner, prisons, and schools. If it be proposed to inculcate some truth, or to foster some feeling by the encouragement of a great example, they form a society.[2]

Tocqueville also observed that these associations had the great added benefit of enlarging the hearts of their members by drawing otherwise isolated individuals out of their own private preoccupations and narrow interests to participate in something larger than themselves. In the process they learned to work with other citizens, cooperating, compromising and deliberating together in common enterprises. For Tocqueville, this was a great school for learning the civic virtues essential to the success of democracy. 'In democratic countries,' he wrote, 'the science of association is the mother of science; the progress of all the rest depends upon the progress it has made.'[3]

Tocqueville was a liberal in the classical nineteenth-century sense, like his friend John Stuart Mill. Both worried that the power of the modern democratic state and the advent of mass society might weaken the spirit of free association and voluntarism that flourished so well in small-town America. He admired American democracy but stressed that its health was directly proportionate to the strength of its civil society associations, which were threatened by broad social and political trends that Tocqueville perceived were emerging at the time.

By the twenty-first century the large reserve of 'social capital', as we now call it, that Tocqueville saw as a hallmark of early American life has largely dried up. That, at least, is the conclusion of the American political scientist Robert Putnam, 'the Tocqueville of our generation', in his bestselling study *Bowling Alone: The Collapse and Revival of American Community* (2000). Putnam looked at a broad range of US data such as the General Social Survey about membership and participation in civic organisations and traditional voluntary associations that involve direct, face-to-face activity, such as the Boy Scouts, the Lions, the Elks, the Shriners, the Jaycees, the Masons, the Red Cross, the League of Women Voters and local sports clubs, among many others. He also examined statistics on voter turnout, church attendance and trade union membership. It all pointed towards the same disheartening conclusion – that 'the vibrancy of American civil society has notably declined over the past several decades'. Like

Tocqueville, Putnam connected this vibrancy to the strength of civic virtue, social capital and public trust, all of which he considers essential to the health of democracy, just as his French predecessor had in the 1830s. The decline of civil society therefore has a negative impact on politics and general prosperity, which largely depend on the strength of voluntary associational life, even when the latter isn't directly political itself. Putnam's work sounded a Tocquevillian alarm about the atrophy of civic life in contemporary America and its damaging implications for democracy.

In an earlier book, *Making Democracy Work: Civic Tradition in Modern Italy* (1993), Putnam attributed the relative political and economic success of northern Italy compared to the south to the presence of strong, well-established, informal bonds between citizens, such as guilds, social clubs, church groups and community networks, that foster trust and civic involvement, making the region democratically successful and economically prosperous. In southern Italy, by contrast, Putnam found much weaker 'horizontal' bonds between citizens than in the north, but much stronger 'vertical' connections between local elites and their clients in a semi-feudal structure that did not facilitate the same degree of trust and social capital, making it much less successful than the north. Putnam's concern is that the US in the second half of the twentieth century looks increasingly like southern rather than northern Italy, which the *moeurs* of Tocqueville's America more closely resembled.

It was ostensibly concern about the health of British civic life that led Prime Minister David Cameron to promise voters in the 2010 UK general election that, if elected, a Conservative government would make the active promotion and strengthening of civil society a matter of government policy, which appears to miss the very point of civil society. To this end, an Office for Civil Society was created to oversee this policy, promoting localism and volunteerism. Cynics wasted little time pointing out that this policy coincided with large cuts in public spending, raising suspicions that the 'Big Society' idea – as it was labelled – was really just a rationalisation for a 'Small State', a Conservative preoccupation since the era of Margaret Thatcher. If this criticism is true, then the political elevation of civil society is really just another neoliberal attempt to shift welfare from the state to charitable groups without addressing deeper problems of structural poverty and low expectations.

Cameron's intellectual guru at the time was Phillip Blond, who provided the theory behind the 'Big Society' idea. This slogan refers to the 'civic middle in British public life – the self-organised associations such as unions, churches and activist organisations' that Blond claims have been gradually killed off by the rise of the Big Market of monopoly capitalism and the Big State of welfarist social democracy.[4] He waxes nostalgic for what the conservative statesman Edmund Burke called the 'little platoons' that had traditionally constituted the social life of England – small, local, 'reciprocal social relationships, through

127

friendships, contacts, families, groups, neighbourliness, political membership, sports teams and churches' – that Blond believes are the key to social contentment and human well-being.[5] He shares Tocqueville's faith in localism and the spontaneous intermediary associations that once flourished in the space between a modest, restrained state and a market consisting mainly of small family businesses, farms and cottage industries.

According to Blond, when liberalism develops unchecked it creates 'a new and wholly terrifying tyranny' that destroys civil society by allowing the growth of giant market monopolies and a leviathan welfare state. These two oppressive millstones have, between them, ground down the independence and authenticity that Blond believes once defined life when society was 'big'. His antidote to these pathologies, like Tocqueville's, is 'the revival of the associative society', a new 'Big Society' rich with voluntary groups that support and strengthen social bonds free of state coercion and corporate power, where individuals can express themselves spontaneously and freely.[6] Economically, Blond is sympathetic to Catholic social teaching and distributivist ideas that seek to disperse ownership as widely as possible throughout society by means of worker-controlled cooperatives, small businesses and mutual societies of the kind that flourished in nineteenth-century and early twentieth-century Britain.

The writer and academic Roger Scruton was another contemporary 'civil society conservative' who situated himself in a tradition of thinkers sceptical of state power, such as Adam

Smith, Edmund Burke, Thomas Jefferson and Friedrich Hayek. He wrote, echoing Tocqueville, that 'it is not the state but civil society – the free association between individuals – that contains the solution to the pressing collective problems, and therefore that it is not state control but individual liberty that is needed by a great society for its success'.[7] Conservatives like Scruton and Blond believe that the established customs and traditions that they value tend to grow naturally from the rich soil of civil society according to 'their own inner dynamic, outside the control of the state', in Scruton's words.[8] States that are in the grip of political ideologies often pose a grave risk to these organic traditions, which don't fit the neat, abstract designs of theorists and social reformers. This is how Scruton interpreted the history of twentieth-century communism, which he argued had forced traditional conservatism and classical liberalism together in a 'symbiotic' relationship, as they both believed in individual liberty as the 'ultimate political value' and this was threatened above all by communism. He became personally involved in helping dissident academics in communist Czechoslovakia in the 1980s, which led to him being placed on its Index of Undesirable Persons there and eventually expelled from that country.

The admiration that Tocqueville and Putnam professed for early American civil society was shared by Scruton, who depicted it as a nation 'built from below, through the free association of its citizens', something that offers 'scope for conservatism as a philosophy of civil society'.[9] Yet we know from Putnam's own research that, by the time Scruton wrote these words, American civil society was in deep crisis. Blond claims that the unlimited state and the unrestrained market have, between them, 'destroyed civil society'. So it is not at all clear how we are to get from no society to a 'Big Society', assuming we wanted to.

The conservative American political theorist Patrick Deneen's recent critique of liberalism strongly echoes Blond and Scruton, including their lack of clarity about how we are meant to regrow civil society in an age of advanced technology, rampant consumerism and overpowering multinational corporations. He is a Tocquevillian nostalgic for the early America of small towns, a limited state and thick, religiously based community that so impressed the great French aristocrat in the 1830s. Like Blond, Deneen sees both the liberal state and capitalist markets as culprits in the subversion of this ideal world where virtuous simplicity reigned. In fact, he sees states and markets as inextricably connected, aspects of a single hegemonic liberal ideology that is the root of virtually all the social and political problems and pathologies of the present. His account is reminiscent of what the Swiss philosopher Jean-Jacques Rousseau called 'nascent society' – 'the happiest epoch and the most lasting' in the history of humanity, a golden age of simplicity optimally balancing individual and community but doomed not to last and leading, when it begins its inevitable descent, to 'the decrepitude of the species', which is where Deneen appears to see us now.

Deneen argues that modern states and markets have systematically eroded traditional civic associations of community, family and church that are the principal source of our identity, morals and liberty. By dissolving these customary networks that encouraged the self-disciplines and denials necessary for collective life, individuals have become atomised, decadent and dependent on the state and on markets to define them. 'Having shorn people's ties to the vast web of intermediating institutions that sustained them,' he writes, 'the expansion of individualism deprived them of recourse to those traditional places of support and sustenance. The more individuated the polity, the more likely that a mass of individuals would inevitably turn to the state in times of need.'[10] Civil society is therefore of 'paramount importance' to Deneen since only there can the 'arts of association' that are the source of humane civic life be nurtured and sustained.

The modern dilemma is that liberalism has been so successful in destroying traditional life and has so thoroughly 'hollowed out' the institutions of civil society there is very little soil from which to grow a healthy new social world. This has been both the success and the failure of liberalism, according to Deneen, since the situation it has created is socially unsustainable in the long run.

Although we are told that 'the end of liberalism is in sight', Deneen's prescriptions for where we go from here, like Blond's, are disappointingly brief and extremely sketchy. They appear to involve building a new, post-liberal culture from the local level up. Economically, this means developing practices that 'support the flourishing of households but which in turn seek to transform the household into a small economy' based on the skills of 'building, fixing, cooking, planting, preserving'.[11] Politically, it predictably requires a limited government. The essential work of cultivating and sustaining social and moral life will occur naturally and spontaneously within civil society if left free from the interference of states and markets. The latter are a risk to the growth and healthy development of civil society, so need to be contained.

Like other civil society conservatives, Deneen tells us nothing about what role he thinks the state should play today in our world of massive corporate power. His hope and wish appears to be that both will just shrink to their proper, human proportions when liberalism finally collapses under the weight of its own internal contradictions, as it is doomed to, much as Marx expected capitalism to fall from a tree like an overripe fruit, a prediction that was not among his most prescient. Like Marx, Deneen is just waiting for history to do what we are powerless to.

The Social Left

There is a tradition of political thought and action on the left that shares the scepticism about the state found among some classical liberals and conservatives and also looks for inspiration to civil society as the realm of popular, grassroots, community-based democracy. Like its counterparts on the right, the 'social left', as it is sometimes called, shifted its hopes after the collapse of Soviet communism and the growing disillusionment with statist economic policy in the democratic West to the 'third sector' beyond both the market and the state. But it sees this sphere as socially progressive and politically radical rather than liberal or conservative.

This is manifest in radical new social movements such as the student protests across the West in May 1968, Occupy Wall Street, popular anti-austerity movements in Greece and Spain, Antifa, and the successful demonstrations in Cochabamba, Bolivia in 1999–2000 against the privatisation of the city's water supply that united indigenous groups, the urban poor and environmentalists. All are part of a 'global associational revolution'[12] by oppressed and marginalised people and their advocates and supporters, who have risen up to challenge established political and economic elites that dominate both the market and the state. For these groups, formal democratic structures have been appropriated, bought off, and taken over by the rich and powerful, who use them for their own purposes. Change must therefore come from below, outside of formal political structures, rising up spontaneously from local communities and expressing the views and interests of the poor and historically voiceless.

Opposition to the state has deep roots on the left. As mentioned above, Karl Marx viewed the state as the hand-maiden of business, a purely coercive apparatus at the disposal of elites to subdue everyone else, incapable of any positive, constructive action. He thought that the capitalist state was unreformable and irredeemable. It would have to be over-thrown, by violence if necessary. Although Marx spent a great deal of his time and energy engaging in bitter polemics with anarchists, whom he never tired of abusing, his own concep-tion of a future communist society is essentially anarchistic. It will have no state at all; the state will gradually 'wither away', his friend and co-author Friedrich Engels predicted, since no coercion is necessary when capitalism and classes are abolished.

The post-capitalist world Marx sketched is radically liber-tarian, a pure society with no state. His passionate disagree-ments with the revolutionary anarchist Mikhail Bakunin were about how to get there rather than the goal itself. Today, radical free market libertarians, usually regarded as on the 'right', have a much more Marxist view of the state than most socialists or social democrats do, despite being regarded as on the 'left'. Yet again we are let down by our outdated political vocabulary when labelling such ideas.

One of the most influential proponents of libertarian socialism today is the American anarchist Noam Chomsky, whose deeply hostile view of the state he traces back to early classical liberalism, epitomised by the German writer Wilhelm von Humboldt, an ideology he thinks has much in common with the early Marx. Chomsky argues that the core of classical liberalism is 'opposition to all but the most restricted minimal forms of state intervention in personal or social life',[13] something that it shares with anarchism. Indeed, he claims that anarchism is 'the development of the remnants of classical liberalism and conversion of them into ways of thinking and acting in a capitalist or post-capitalist society'.[14] Chomsky draws a direct line from classical liberalism to libertarian socialism, which he depicts as essentially the application of classical liberal thinking to an age of industrial capitalism.

According to Chomsky, with the advent of modern industrial capitalism, liberalism disastrously allied itself with the state, so that today it has little, if anything, in common with the early, pre-capitalist classical liberalism of von Humboldt. Chomsky shares Marx's view that the state is nothing but the servant of capitalism, the 'shadow cast on society by big business', to borrow John Dewey's phrase.[15] In fact, today it is corporate power that is 'by far the most dangerous of all',[16] a form of private tyranny that is so great even the anarchist Chomsky thinks the state may legitimately be used as a check on it. Nor does he consider the Soviet state to have been truly socialist. He denounced it as a betrayal of libertarian socialism no less than modern 'state-capitalism' is a betrayal of the humanistic ideals of early, classical liberalism. In neither system do workers control the means of production, and therefore neither system is really free.

Although Chomsky's social ideal is anarchist, he regards the abolition of the state in present circumstances as simply utopian since there's nothing to replace it. 'To talk about eliminating the state in the world as it exists', he claims with admirable realism, 'is simply to keep yourself in some remote academic seminar.'[17] However, he has been encouraged by some grass-roots activism and popular democratic protest movements that have sprung up from the social soil among those with little or no voice in established systems of public authority. This has been particularly true since the fall of socialist states in the East and the rise of the business-friendly neoliberal state in the West.

The large and sometimes violent protests against the WTO meeting in Seattle, Washington in 1999 attracted a broad assortment of students, labour unions, environmentalists, anarchists and religious groups demonstrating against the policies of international financial institutions for damaging the environment and harming the poor, particularly in the developing world. The Seattle protests raised the profile of these issues and inspired others to support them, both worthwhile achievements. But they did little to loosen the iron grip of neoliberalism on the world over the longer term. The same is true of the 2011 Occupy Wall Street protest in New York City. It was a similar coalition of disparate social groups opposed to corporate wealth and power, although its bohemian supporters are probably not quite what conservatives like Phillip Blond, Roger Scruton and Patrick Deneen have in mind for a revitalised civil society. Occupy Wall Street relied on social media, word-of-mouth and a poster campaign to generate support under the slogan 'We are the 99%'. Although the protest attracted a lot of media attention and was, like Seattle, symbolically important, its lack of specific policy demands meant it produced no real change to the economic system it opposed. Eventually the protesters were forced out of their makeshift base in Zuccotti Park in New York's finan-cial district and the movement gradually faded away.

The World Social Forum (WSF) is an annual meeting of diverse civil society organisations that first convened in Brazil in 2001 at the same time as the World Economic Forum held its annual meeting of the rich and powerful in Davos, Switzerland. The WSF is an 'anti-Davos' gathering that began with the slogan 'Another world is possible' in opposition to the pro-business poli-cies of the world's political and economic elites. But it has been increasingly criticised for lacking substance and coherence, a common problem for loose, broad-based, grassroots movements. It has also become increasingly dominated by non-governmental organisations (NGOs). These are non-profit, voluntary bodies formally independent of government that promote humani-tarian causes, consumer protection, environmental safeguards, undertake fundraising for charity, lobby businesses and govern-ments, organise aid, and gather and disseminate information. There are estimated to be over ten million NGOs worldwide today. The vast majority are national, and around forty thousand operate internationally, leading some to talk about an emergent new global civil society.[18] Many of the largest and most influential NGOs, such as Oxfam, the Red Cross, BRAC, the Ford Foundation, the Gates Foundation, Save the Children, Médecins Sans Frontières and Care International, have relationships or official associative status with intergovernmental organisations such as the United Nations and the World Bank.

Ideally, NGOs, like other civil society groups, would support popular, bottom-up democracy and popular government. Sometimes that ideal is realised in practice, but NGOs have their own interests, agendas and outlook that sometimes diverge from disadvantaged or marginalised groups who are meant to be their beneficiaries. In recent years an increasing amount of charity and foreign development aid has been channelled through NGOs rather than directly to national governments, which are often perceived as corrupt or inefficient. This has led to a massive proliferation in their numbers and made them much more reliant on international funding than in the past. Much of this money comes from governments, international agencies and wealthy donors in the West who expect to set priorities and add conditions to their donations, undercutting the NGO's independence and weakening democratic decision-making in the recipient countries. Accountability can be a problem when NGOs are dependent on a small number of wealthy donors to whom they feel answerable, rather than to the people they are meant to be helping. Secrecy is also a problem since NGOs aren't always transparent in how they make policies and allocate their resources. Their leaders are not normally elected and they employ many professionals and bureaucrats who are unaccountable to local communities or voters. They may have little knowledge or real understanding of the people they are trying to help and are often apt to dominate them. To impoverished locals they may appear indistinguishable from the foreign corporate investors looking to buy up their land and resources.

This 'NGO-isation' of civil society has led to accusations that they are now 'the handmaidens of capitalist change'[19] and a form of neo-colonialism. For this reason many developing countries have passed laws limiting foreign funding of NGOs. A 2013 study published in the *Journal of Democracy* found that 'Of our 98 countries, 51 either prohibit (12) or restrict (39) foreign funding of civil society. Even if we assume that all countries for which we have no information are free (which is highly unlikely), at least 26 percent of the UN's 193 member states limit foreign funding for NGOs.'[20] This trend is not surprising, since states in the developing world often perceive NGOs as undercutting their independence and legitimacy, a means by which foreign interests can bypass them to directly impose their own policies.

Many popular social movements are deeply suspicious of governments and stress their autonomy from both state and capital. This is true in much of Latin America, where marginalised, anti-establishment civil society groups have often faced brutally authoritarian governments. The ideological roots of the Mexican Zapatistas, for example, are in agrarian socialism and anarchism. They are named for Emiliano Zapata, who led a popular revolution against the Mexican state in 1910. The brief neo-Zapatista uprising in the traditionally poor Chiapas region of southern Mexico in 1994 was provoked by concerns about the effect of the North American Free Trade Agreement on local farmers. This has inspired other groups in South and Central America who feel themselves to be victims of global capitalism sold out by business-friendly governments. The popular protests in Cochabamba, Bolivia in 1999 mentioned above are a good example. The government there had been pressured into this by the IMF in exchange for 'structural adjustment loans' that it needed. Almost immediately the privatised water company dramatically raised prices, hitting the poor hardest. The protests brought together many local community groups who successfully fought the 'Cochabamba Water War' to reverse the privatisation of their water.

Uncivil Society

These civil society groups and protest movements may win some local battles, like the Cochabambas, but they will not win the war against the present economic system, at least for now and for the foreseeable future. If civil society as a realm of individual freedom, democratic cooperation and spontaneous community action did once exist, it no longer does. We inhabit a world where the market has almost completely colonised what is called 'civil society', which is now saturated with advertising and dominated by commercialism that undermine both individuality and authentic community. Civil society is not part of an autonomous 'third sector' independent of state and market; it *is* the market now.

Tocqueville lived before the advent of industrial capitalism, when the US was an overwhelmingly rural, agricultural Protestant society. He quaintly praised newspapers at the time as a form of communication that could bind together groups free of government control. Tocqueville never imagined that, by 2014, the average American adult would consume almost ten hours of media per day.[21] Nor was it within his comprehension in the 1830s to foresee how completely dominated our lives would become by commercial advertising. When Robert Putnam came to survey American civic life 150 years later things looked very different from Tocqueville's America, and to Putnam's eyes very much worse. He blamed the individualising of our leisure time through television and the internet for a substantial part of the loss of civic engagement in America since the 1970s.

Businesses worldwide now spend over $500 billion a year to promote their goods and services, enveloping us in a pervasive, often smothering, atmosphere of advertising. Adverts constantly appear not only in commercials on television, radio, cinemas and the internet, but in video games, magazines, on clothing, billboards, flags, the sides of buildings, buses, taxis, sporting venues, schools, metros and even police cars. Basically every-thing. There are special commercial patient channels in some hospitals now. Product placement in films and on television has long been routine, blurring the boundary between adver-tising and programming. Sports stadiums have been named (or renamed) for commercial sponsors, such as Cardiff's Principality Stadium, Toronto's Rogers Centre, Stuttgart's Mercedes-Benz Arena and the HSH Nordbank Arena in Hamburg, to name just a few. Airports and metro stations are now crammed with shops and saturated by commercial advertising. Our urban spaces in particular are almost wholly dominated by marketing and retail sales and so commodified that they have virtually no function left but to buy and sell goods.

According to one study (from 2014), a typical American adult has between three thousand and twenty thousand 'brand exposures' per day, meaning they pass by that number of brand names, images, commercial products or labels of all kinds daily, although they will be conscious of very few of them. This includes about 360 actual adverts we each see on average every day across all media, which is over 130,000 per year.[22]

Exposure to this constant barrage starts very early. Most American children now have a television in their bedroom and own mobile phones and computers, which is one reason there is so much dedicated child-oriented programming and advertising today. In 2000, the American Psychological Association Task Force on Advertising and Children found that the average American child watches more than forty thousand television commercials a year. It also concluded that children under the age of seven to eight years 'do not recognise the persuasive intent of commercial appeals'. This makes them extremely vulnerable to the manipulative power of advertising, which they tend to accept uncritically since they don't perceive it as advertising.[23] While some jurisdictions have begun to impose restrictions on advertising aimed at children, they are still very much the exception. Young minds that are still forming and are highly impressionable are being relentlessly bombarded with advertising, much of it designed for and directed at their age group. They are turned into consumers long before they become citizens.

The intensity and reach of modern advertising have been massively enhanced by recent advances in science and technology, such as smartphones, computers, satellites, televisions, apps, tracking devices and mass media. Advertisers also now avail themselves of the latest research in behavioural psychology, cognitive neuroscience and anthropology to study consumer behaviour and maximise their power to affect it. The field of consumer neuroscience or 'neuromarketing' emerged in the early 2000s to employ new neuroscience tools to improve the ability of corporations to influence consumers. Some companies even have their own laboratories to undertake such research, and others fund academic studies in universities to expand their power over our tastes and spending habits. There is even a Neuromarketing Science and Business Association (NMSBA).

While traditional marketing techniques such as self-reports, questionnaires and interviews are still widely used, new, sophisticated neuroscience technology enables researchers to measure physiological and neurophysiological activity in subjects to gauge their response to marketing stimuli such as advertising and brand recognition and to measure neural activity while consumers engage in consumption-related behaviour.[24] Among these tools are electroencephalography (EEG), eye-tracking (ET), functional magnetic resonance imaging (fMRI), functional near-infrared spectroscopy (fNIRS), facial expression recognition software (fERS), facial electromyography (fEMG), electrocardiography (ECG), galvanic skin response (GSR), voice pitch analysis (VOPAN), positron emission tomography (PET), magnetoencephalography (MEG), transcranial magnetic stimulation (TMS) and steady-state topography (SST). With these means at their disposal scientists can measure a wide range of voluntary and involuntary reflexes such as heart rate, respiration rate, blood circulation, blood pressure, sweating and oxygen flows to the brain and reflex responses such as gaze fixation and pupil dilation. This knowledge has enabled advertisers to refine techniques for triggering emotional responses in consumers, influencing unconscious biases and preferences, and manipulating our innate mental dispositions and appetites. The harmless-sounding word 'advertising' today masks a very sophisticated and quite insidious system of science-based manipulation that we rarely consciously perceive. It doesn't just seek to persuade us to prefer brand 'X' over brand 'Y'; it aims to implant in us desires for products where none existed before.

One example of this is our growing understanding of how repetition encourages belief. Our minds find it increasingly difficult to distinguish what is true from what is familiar over time. While this is not itself a new discovery ('Sixty-two thousand four hundred repetitions make one truth', Aldous Huxley wrote in his prophetic 1932 novel *Brave New World*), our understanding of why this is so has increased greatly, as has our appreciation of just how strong this tendency is, which advertisers use to induce us to spend. The convincing explanation for this repetition effect provided by Nobel-winning behavioural economist Daniel Kahneman is that our brains operate two parallel systems, one fast, subconscious and emotional ('system 1'), the other slow, conscious and more rational ('system 2'). When processing information and making decisions we often rely on cognitive shortcuts via system 1, since it is faster and easier, if sloppier and not as reliable as system 2. Advertisers, who are well aware of all this, focus their attention on system 1, which is much more easily misled and manipulated than system 2.[25]

Advertisers also rely on priming, the phenomenon whereby one stimulus influences a response to another because of their unconscious association in our minds. A small example Kahneman gives of 'the marvels of priming' occurs when you see or hear the word 'eat'. Studies have shown that most people, having first seen this word, are more likely to complete the word fragment SO_P as SOUP rather than SOAP. The implications of this realisation for advertising are enormous. It enables advertisers to subtly trigger positive and negative reactions in consumers to influence their choices, usually without us ever noticing. Much advertising today is about creating these emotional connections. For example, advertisers now use 'cause-related marketing' where they deliberately link their product to a socially worthy cause to increase its appeal, particularly to specific demographic groups known to purchase or consume the product. This has recently expanded into the phenomenon of 'Woke Capitalism' as major multinational brands openly associate themselves with politically progressive causes, which they often fund and promote, at least partly to win the approval of consumers and, thereby, increase sales, as well as to improve their public image.

Businesses also employ framing, which is a cognitive bias where people decide on options based on whether they are presented with positive or negative connotations, such as a loss or a gain. People tend to avoid risk when a positive frame is presented but seek risks when a negative frame is presented. Knowing this, advertisers can manipulate consumers into making choices by deliberately 'framing' their options without them knowing. There are many such cognitive biases that have been demonstrated by experimental psychologists, most of them associated with what Kahneman calls our fast, unconscious 'system 1' brain. Businesses now make extensive use of such knowledge when designing, timing, targeting and positioning advertising.

An environment like this inevitably produces more standardisation than variety. The many diverse 'little platoons' of civil society that are meant to shoot up from the soil of freedom end up looking, acting and sounding increasingly alike, which was precisely the fate that Tocqueville feared for America. He hoped that a strong and vibrant civil society that fosters independence and invention would offset the homogenising force of mass society. But today, civil society *is* mass society in much of the world.

The generally benevolent view of civil society that is widely shared by many on the left and the right today who are suspicious of state power often overlooks or understates just how uncivil it can be. Most voluntary groups are 'member-serving' rather than 'public-service'; they exist to promote their own particular interests. This may be perfectly benign, as in the case of a seniors' club or choral society, but it can also encourage what David Rieff calls the 'the new medievalism of civil society',[26] a social fragmentation and tribalism of groups with competing interests and identities. Many civil society associations are essentially private clubs with exclusive attitudes and membership. This tendency has been greatly exacerbated by the internet and social media, which often cause 'siloing' of groups and opinions and can encourage partisan extremism and polarisation.[27] Little wonder it causes so much misery.[28]

Those who place their hope in 'civil society' as the path to a better world today are fooling themselves. They romanticise it as a realm of freedom, popular democracy and voluntary association. That may have been true in the small towns of 1830s New England, and among the early friendly societies, cooperatives and mutual aid organisations of the nineteenth century before the welfare state, and in the communist states of 1980s Eastern Europe, but it is not true today. The forms of private power that dominate our world now, enormously magnified by modern science and technology, have penetrated all aspects of life to such an extent that the sphere we call 'civil society' has largely become a thing of the past.

6

STATE CAPITALISM: FROM WASHINGTON TO BEIJING

The changing status of Britain's rail system, which has moved from private ownership to public, back to private and now to semi-public, reflects changing attitudes towards the market and the state. In 2021 the British government of Boris Johnson announced that the country's privately owned rail network would be partly renationalised under a new company to be patriotically called 'Great British Railways'. This body will assume responsibility for the rail track, stations, ticketing, time-tables and network planning, although disappointingly the trains themselves will still be run by private companies.

This is a partial retreat from the privatisation of Britain's railway system by the government of John Major in the mid-1990s, one of the last of a wave of sell-offs of British public companies begun by his predecessor, Margaret Thatcher. Major broke up and sold off 'British Rail' to private franchises, although several of these are now actually owned by foreign, state-owned firms like the German national rail company Deutsche Bahn, which owns Arriva Trains. So some of the UK's rail system has remained in public hands, just not in British hands. As a result, British rail passengers are helping to fund public rail companies in other countries.

The privatisation of Britain's rail system was very controversial when it began in 1994 and has remained so ever since. Popular opinion has consistently favoured returning it to public ownership.[1] Privatisation never really opened the system up to market competition anyway. Instead, it created a series of regional monopolies that are subsidised by British taxpayers. But it did provide the government with a windfall to spend on other things and to cut taxes.

The pendulum between public and private power is constantly swinging, as I have already recounted in earlier chapters. It is now just beginning to swing back towards the state, raising the possibility that the drastic neoliberal swing towards the market that began in the 1970s is finally about to be corrected.

One reason for these swings is that capitalism itself is always changing. It is not a fixed entity. It comes in many different forms and can be highly adaptive. The intense competition of early industrial capitalism gave way to oligopoly and monopoly capitalism, where there is little real competition. The old, competitive capitalism of the early nineteenth century based on the export of goods was succeeded by the new, monopolistic form of capitalism that emerged in the late nineteenth and early twentieth centuries based largely on the export of capital. After the postwar experiment with 'controlled capitalism', we returned to a system of loosely regulated, oligopolistic capitalism dominated by mammoth private multinational corporations. But this form of capitalism has provoked a backlash and is increasingly challenged by a new form – state capitalism. The partial renationalisation of Britain's railways should be seen in this larger context, as part, albeit a very small part, of a general transition that is beginning from neoliberalism to a more active state involvement in economic life. Few politicians today recognise this profound shift or, if they do, are willing to discuss it openly. But eventually they will have to, and the sooner the better.

This process is being spearheaded from Beijing, the leading practitioner of state capitalism today, along with Russia and Saudi Arabia. Since the mid-2000s Chinese leaders have reversed economic reforms launched in the 1990s by tightening government management of leading companies, strategically steering them according to its long-term priorities, and shaping corporate agendas. This trend is also apparent in many other countries, including in the West, as in the case of Britain's railways, although not on anything like the same scale as in China. These changes have led some to speak of the emergence of 'a new era of state capitalism'.[2]

Public Interest Capitalism?

Leon Trotsky once wryly observed that the term state capitalism has the polemical advantage that 'nobody knows exactly what it means'. It remains true that there is no generally agreed definition. However, any reasonable definition must include a leading role for the state in the economy and the existence of state-owned enterprises (SOEs) that operate in the marketplace. Political scientist Joshua Kurlantzick, an expert on the subject, distinguishes state capitalism today from previous forms of state ownership since now it 'combines statist strategies with aspects of free-market multinationals in a far more sophisticated manner than the twentieth century's type of state capitalism'.[3]

What counts as a state-owned enterprise is also essentially contested. For example, the 2020 Fortune Global 500 list of companies refers to the Chinese defence and aeronautics business Aviation Industry Corporation of China (AVIC) as a 'private' business, even though it is regarded by almost all experts as state-owned and is under the supervision of the State-Owned Assets Supervision and Administration Commission (SASAC), China's powerful commission that oversees the country's largest SOEs. Sometimes an enterprise is classed as state-owned if the government holds, either directly or indirectly, over a certain percentage of its equity capital, say 25 per cent. But there is no agreed level, so any such definition is likely to be arbitrary and therefore disputable. A reasonable compromise definition of an SOE might be one in which the state is the largest stakeholder, giving it effective control, even if its share is below 50 per cent.

SOEs differ from private corporations in not necessarily having profit maximisation as their sole objective or *raison d'être*. Instead, most trade off some profit for other public policy objectives, such as protecting jobs or safeguarding strategic national interests. For example, a state-owned airline may schedule flights to remote communities which are unprofitable but promote a social good by providing vital transportation links that in a free market would lose money and therefore likely not exist. This may be why, according to some studies (disputed by others), SOEs are generally less profitable than their private counterparts.[4] This is a decisive difference between private businesses and SOEs, since the former will always pursue profit over other goods.

Another difference is that the profits of SOEs, if there are any, can be used by the state to improve public services, fund pensions and invest in infrastructure. For example, the giant Norwegian oil company Equinor is 67 per cent owned by the Norwegian state, which receives regular dividends from it, expected to be 8.7 billion Norwegian kroner (US$1 billion) in 2021 for a population of 5.4 million people.[5] This money is transferred to the Government Pension Fund Global, the world's largest sovereign wealth fund, established to invest surplus revenues from the country's petroleum sector, according to the Sovereign Wealth Fund Institute. Money from this fund can be used by the government to finance important public goods without drawing on its capital. In May 2021 the fund was worth $1.3 trillion, or $248,000 for every man, woman and child in Norway.[6]

Russia's National Wealth Fund is ranked by the Sovereign Wealth Fund Institute as the fourteenth largest in the world with total assets of $186 billion. It receives profits from its many investments, including the country's huge state-owned oil and gas companies such as Gazprom, the largest publicly listed gas firm in the world, and Rosneft. Like Equinor in Norway, these SOEs usually generate billions of dollars in profits annually, much of which is paid in dividends to Russia's National Wealth Fund to provide the Russian government with extra revenues. In 2021 the government announced that it would spend up to 400 billion roubles ($5.5 billion) annually from the fund to boost state investment in infrastructure projects and finance its national development strategy.[7]

Air Singapore is majority owned by Temasek Holdings, a holding company whose sole shareholder is Singapore's Ministry of Finance. Temasek has a large and diverse range of investments beyond Air Singapore, with total assets of $484.44 billion, making it the world's seventh-largest sovereign wealth fund.[8] It pays an annual dividend to the Singapore government which amounts to over 20 per cent of its yearly revenues.

Emirates Airlines, the fourth largest in the world, is owned by the Investment Corporation of Dubai, another state-owned sovereign wealth fund, ranked tenth in the world with total assets of $302.33 billion. Like Temasek, the fund invests in a wide range of businesses and generates a substantial annual profit for the government of Dubai.

In all these cases, and there are over fifty sovereign wealth funds in the world today, profits enrich the public coffers rather than lining the pockets of wealthy shareholders or paying for bonuses and perks to corporate managers.

SOEs that are democratically accountable are also more likely than private corporations to adopt a 'double bottom line', factoring the social and environmental impact of their activities into their calculations, rather than just the standard, single bottom line of financial profit and loss. This is particularly true in areas that enjoy wide popular support. Since they are backed by the state, they are more likely to tolerate lower profits in exchange for social goods, which is a good trade-off that plays no significant part in the calculations of private corporations.[9]

The number of SOEs in the world has expanded rapidly in the last twenty years. According to the Fortune Global 500 list of the world's largest companies (by revenue), the twenty-seven SOEs in 2000 (5.4 per cent of the world's top 500 companies) had increased to 110 by 2020 (22 per cent). Of these 110 SOEs in 2020, eighty-four were Chinese, or 76 per cent, compared to just nine Chinese SOEs out of twenty-seven in their 2000 list, or 33 per cent. Of the SOEs outside China, twelve are in OECD countries and fourteen are not. In 2020 SOEs accounted for US$8 trillion, or 24 per cent of the total company revenue of Fortune's Global 500 list. So the dramatic rise of large state-owned enterprises in the global economy is due overwhelmingly to China. Countries with the highest concentration of SOEs among their top firms are China (96 per cent), the United Arab Emirates (88 per cent), Russia (82 per cent), Indonesia (69 per cent) and Malaysia (68 per cent). Geographically, China has the largest SOE sector overall (51,000 firms), followed by Hungary (370), India (270), Brazil (134), the Czech Republic (133), Lithuania (128), Poland (126) and the Slovak Republic (113).

SOEs tend to be concentrated in certain sectors, such as finance and capital-intensive, large-scale strategic areas like natural resources, energy and heavy industries. The high risks and huge costs associated with these sectors often deter private investors, who are frequently highly risk-averse unless they are 'too-big-to-fail' banks. Five of the ten largest oil and gas companies in the world today are publicly owned (Sinopec, China National Petroleum Corporation, PetroChina, Saudi Aramco, Rosneft) and three-quarters of the world's known oil reserves are now controlled by state-owned companies.[10] The largest of these state-owned energy companies are larger than their massive private counterparts such as ExxonMobil, Royal Dutch Shell, Chevron, BP and Total. The electricity and gas, transportation, telecoms and other utilities sectors account for 51 per cent of all SOEs by value and 70 per cent by employment.

The financial sector also has a high concentration of SOEs, mainly in China.[11] According to the S&P Global Market Intelligence Report 2020, the 'Big Four' state-owned Chinese banks are the four largest banks in the world. China is also home to the greatest number of top one hundred global banks, with nineteen institutions together owning assets of US$25.81 trillion, although not all of these are state-owned.[12]

The global economy is dividing into two different capitalisms, one privately owned and run on broadly neoliberal lines and the other publicly owned and state-capitalist. States and markets co-exist everywhere today. They need each other. Political and ideological debate now is almost entirely over how much of each, state and market, is best, ranging from 'minarchists', who prefer an ultra-minimal state confined to basic police functions, to those who favour a very strong and active state that plays a commanding role in the economy and provides a full range of welfare services to its citizens. We are now in a time of increasing divergence on the balance between public and private power in the world, with the West on one path and the East increasingly on another.

This species of giant state-owned corporation is not simply a reversion to socialism of the kind that existed in the Soviet Union or in Maoist China. Socialism is usually defined as a system where the means of production, such as factories, natural resources, technology and capital, are owned by workers or on their behalf by a proletarian state with a planned economy. State-owned enterprises, by contrast, operate in markets and compete directly with private businesses. Almost all states today, even in neoliberal capitalist systems, have some SOEs, although they are much more common in the developing world than in the West.

For the most part, Western governments have used the state to support and regulate the market and to step in with bailouts when they fail, or appear about to fail. Such states plug gaps in markets and limit some of their excesses, sometimes. This 'market failure' approach may involve some amount of temporary state ownership of corporations. For example, the UK government bailed out several failing banks in 2008 and 2009 with massive loans, share purchases and guarantees. In the process it acquired a large majority stake in the Royal Bank of Scotland. Western states are primarily reactive and don't set long-term strategic goals for the economy, which is guided by market forces according to neoliberal ideology.

The situation in China is very different, and increasingly so. For a time, its Communist government began to steer a course in the direction of Western neoliberalism. Major economic reforms were instituted by Premier Zhu Rongji between 1998 and 2003. In the wake of the Asian financial crisis in 1997 he privatised many mid-sized and small SOEs at the local and provincial level and significantly reduced the size of China's vast state bureaucracy. Many state-owned companies went bankrupt while foreign direct investment into China rose rapidly. The number of industrial SOEs in China declined from 64,700 in 1998 to 20,300 in 2010 and SOE workers decreased by almost half between 1993 and 2004.[13] The government also tightened credit terms for businesses during these years. This liberalisation policy was partly intended to prepare China for admission to the World Trade Organization, which it joined in 2001.

However, since Rongji's departure from office in 2003, Beijing has gradually changed tack away from neoliberalism. That year the Chinese government set up the State-Owned Assets Supervision and Administration Commission under its State Council to manage the country's many state-owned enterprises. The combined assets of these ninety-five businesses now exceed US$25 trillion, making the SASAC the largest economic entity in the world. In the mid-1990s, SOEs made up about 10 per cent of China's annual GDP; by the mid-2010s this had risen to 25 per cent.[14] By 2012 SOEs owned 66 per cent of all assets in China.[15] Fourteen of the sixteen largest Chinese companies operating outside China are SOEs and over 90 per cent of Chinese outward investment derives from such companies.[16] The central government owns 51,000 SOEs of varying sizes, employing twenty million people.[17] This includes the world's four largest banks based on total assets, according to S&P,[18] and the three largest oil and gas companies (Sinopec, State Grid and China National Petroleum) by revenue, according to the 2020 Fortune Global 500, where ninety-one of China's 124 largest firms are SOEs.

In 2020, for the first time since it began publishing its annual list twenty years earlier, China had the largest number of companies represented in the Fortune Global 500, 124 compared to 121 US firms. In a distant third place was Japan, with just fifty-three companies. China now has more firms on the Fortune list than France, Germany and the UK combined. Together the US and China now account for almost half of all Fortune Global 500 companies. This is a striking change from just two decades ago, when China had only ten companies in the top 500. The US has trended in the other direction, with 179 companies in 2000 and 139 in 2010. A large majority of these top-500 Chinese enterprises are state-owned, whereas none of the US companies are.

China's State Council SASAC, which manages the country's SOEs, appoints their managers and directors and makes decisions about large investments such as mergers and the sale of major assets. The China Development Bank, created in 1994, also operates under the State Council. It supports strategic development of the Chinese economy according to the policies of the government, mainly by funding large-scale infrastructure projects, particularly in basic industries, transportation, communications and energy, such as the massive Three Gorges Dam, the world's largest power station. And the Chinese Communist Party's secretive Organisation Department controls millions of positions in government and industry, enabling it to achieve maximum conformity to its national economic policies.

Beijing's increasingly active involvement in China's economy has accelerated under Xi Jinping, who became president in 2013. He has repeatedly warned against following Western economic and political models and has taken China in another direction, sometimes called the 'China model' or a new 'Beijing Consensus' to rival the dominant neoliberal 'Washington Consensus'. Private firms are still allowed to operate in China, where the vast majority of goods and services are bought and sold in markets that are relatively free from government control or subsidy. In 2014 there were over forty-one million private businesses in China, a fivefold increase since 2006.[19] Even so, state enterprises account for about a third of all capital spending in China, according to a report by GK Dragonomics, whereas in most developed economies state companies account for no more than 5 per cent. And, as we have seen, most of China's biggest businesses are state-owned enterprises. Many of the leading private multinational companies headquartered in OECD countries now struggle to compete with China's top SOEs.

The Chinese state's economic reach extends to private businesses as well. Many of its SOEs own shares in such companies. For example, the state-owned food and beverages giant Bright Food, headquartered in Shanghai, has at times owned a majority of the New Zealand-based dairy producer Synlait, the dairy and meat company Silver Fern Farms, British cereal brand Weetabix, Australian-based food producer Manassen

Foods, Israeli dairy producer Tnuva, and Italian olive oil producer Salov. Most Chinese investment in US industries is by SOEs. Also, like all states, the government regulates private Chinese businesses, often to a degree that exceeds what is common in the West. Membership of the Communist Party is still likely to be an advantage for executives in private companies, even if it is not a formal requirement. The Chinese government has imposed more restrictions on foreign investment in key sectors of the country's economy to enable domestic businesses to develop, shielded from international competition. In these sectors the government has decreed that the state 'must maintain at least a 50 percent ownership in each firm'.[20] And it has gained access to cutting-edge strategic technologies by enticing many foreign companies into joint ventures with its own firms by tempting them with access to its massive consumer market. By all these methods the Chinese state maintains a paramount position over its economy while still allowing extensive private ownership and markets.

Although China is the leading practitioner of state capitalism in the world today, by far, it is present to a greater or lesser extent over much of the world now, including in the democratic West. Even the United States has publicly owned or funded companies such as the US Postal Service and Amtrak. Huge state-owned corporations such as Equinor (Norway), Petrobras (Brazil), Gazprom (Russia), Rosneft (Russia), Saudi Aramco, Indian Oil, Petronas (Malaysia), National Iranian Oil

Company (NIOC), Petróleos de Venezuela (PDVSA), Pemex (Mexico), Abu Dhabi National Oil Company (United Arab Emirates) and the Kuwait Petroleum Corporation now dominate the world's oil and gas sector, and three-quarters of known oil reserves are controlled by SOEs.[21] In at least twenty-five countries, national oil companies collect revenues equivalent to more than 20 per cent of the government's total revenues.

Many large banks in the developing world today are also state-owned, including China's leading banks such as Industrial and Commercial Bank of China, China Construction Bank, Agricultural Bank of China, Bank of China and China Everbright Bank. Outside China the Banco do Brasil, Caixa Econômica Federal (Brazil), Sberbank (Russia), Janata Bank (Bangladesh), the People's Bank of Sri Lanka, Bank of Ceylon, Krungthai Bank (Thailand), the National Bank of Egypt and Banco de la República Oriental del Uruguay are all state-owned, and many are now among the largest banks in the world.

As we saw in Chapter One, many countries in the twentieth century nationalised key public utilities such as oil and gas, steel, minerals, banking and telecommunications. By the 1970s, public enterprise accounted for an average of 13.5 per cent of capital formation in countries for which investment figures were then available, according to the IMF.[22] The comparison did not include the US, where the figure exceeded 16.5 per cent, or the Soviet Union or China, where it would have been close to, if not actually, 100 per cent.[23] Otherwise, among developed countries the greatest proportions were in Australia, Austria, Canada, Italy, France, Norway, the UK and the Netherlands.[24]

The Entrepreneurial State

The popular image of nationalised industries and state-owned enterprises that was very successfully propagated by neoliberals during their privatisation campaign portrayed them as inefficient white elephants that had become a permanent drain on the national economy. In reality, governments have often actively supported cutting-edge technological innovation which benefits private businesses who are increasingly reluctant to take long-term risks, preferring to focus on immediate profits and pushing up share prices. Many multinational corporations that once engaged in their own ambitious R&D with in-house research centres, such as Bell Labs, Xerox PARC and Alcoa Research Labs, have cut back massively on this once-important work. That is why so much technological risk-taking and innovation has actually been done by states or funded by them, rather than by private enterprises. This is particularly true in the United States, where private entrepreneurs and large, high-profile companies have usually been unfairly credited with risky innovation that was actually undertaken with public money or in public labs. As the political economist Mariana Mazzucato writes in her 2013 study of this phenomenon, *The Entrepreneurial State*, 'despite the perception of the US as the epitome of private sector-led wealth creation, in reality it is the State that has been engaged on a massive scale in entrepreneurial risk taking to spur innovation'.[25]

Mazzucato gives many detailed examples of private companies that have profited from publicly funded research and development which they were initially unwilling to invest in. Apple received early-stage funding from the US government's Small Business Innovation Research Program. She also points out how the pharmaceutical industry has cashed in massively on government-funded research, noting that three-quarters of new molecular biopharmaceutical discoveries owe their creation to publicly funded labs. The cancer drug Taxol, for example, was discovered by a US government agency, the National Institutes of Health, and is now sold by the private pharmaceutical firm Bristol Myers Squibb, one of the largest private corporations in the United States, for a massive profit. And the ubiquitous iPhone, Mazzucato observes, was developed with technologies created in publicly funded labs.[26]

Far from stepping in only when markets fail, but otherwise leaving them to take the lead in technological innovation, Mazzucato shows how 'the State has been key to creating and shaping markets not only "fixing" them'.[27] Like the myth of capitalist competition (Capitalist Myth #1) discussed in Chapter Three, the myth of capitalist innovation (Capitalist Myth

#2) assumes that states exist to correct and regulate markets so they function more effectively, to protect them from their own excesses but otherwise leave them alone to get on with the job of creating new products for consumers. It is this dominant image of the state that is used to justify neoliberal policies intended to get the state out of the way of corporate risk-takers and innovators. Mazzucato argues very convincingly that this image is really a grotesque distortion of reality. A more accurate image, based on the actual history of scientific and technological innovation, would be what she calls the 'entrepreneurial State', which makes its 'courageous risk-taking visionary role' central. The state has long taken a leading part in industrial development and scientific innovation, usually by providing essential support for early-stage, high-risk, strategic research in labs and universities that no longer interest private businesses chasing quarterly profits, although the latter are only too happy to exploit this public investment.

Plutonomy

The executives of many private businesses often complain that SOEs enjoy competitive advantages over their private counterparts, thereby creating an uneven playing field in the market. State funding insulates SOEs from bankruptcy, which non-state businesses face as the ultimate price of failure. But many large private corporations are effectively insulated from bankruptcy as well, and their managers know it. 'Too-big-to-fail' businesses have often been bailed out by governments after engaging in reckless investments that backfired, as in the subprime mortgage crisis in the US. And during the recent Covid pandemic many small and medium-sized private firms benefited from a range of government support, including business grants, tax cuts and deferrals, public equity stakes in some businesses, and loan guarantees.

Another common complaint about SOEs is that they engage in and are subject to political interference. For example, the political appointment by governments of unqualified individuals to the boards of directors of state corporations may create opportunities for political influence in both directions. The American political scientist Ian Bremmer even includes the state use of markets 'primarily for political gain' as part of his definition of state capitalism.[28] It is worth pointing out here that private businesses spend millions of dollars every year around the world lobbying governments to award them contracts and to tailor legislation and regulations in ways favourable to their interests, so they are not in a strong position to object to possible political influence with SOEs.

Like other neoliberal critics of state capitalism, Bremmer also claims that 'in general, the more government intervenes in the process of economic exchange, the more likely it is to burden them with political distortions, bureaucracy, waste, and corruption'.[29] This view, for which he provides virtually no evidence, is an expression of what might be called the myth of capitalist efficiency (Capitalist Myth #3). Compared to their public counterparts, we are told, private businesses are models of efficiency.

So the theory goes. The reality of contemporary capitalism tells a very different story, in which it is highly wasteful, inefficient and frequently unmeritocratic. It is often characterised by weak corporate governance and is dominated by a form of 'managerism', where selfish senior executives at large firms put their own personal interests ahead of the companies they manage, extracting as much from them as they can with few real checks. That is how American CEOs today have ended up being paid around ten times more than their predecessors of the 1960s. Corporate executive pay and bonuses have outpaced corporate profits, economic growth and the average compensation of all workers, particularly since the emergence of the bonus culture in the 1990s.[30] The ratio of CEO compensation to average worker compensation in the US used to be in the region of 30 to 40 to 1 in the 1960s and 1970s. This ratio has grown at a rapid rate since the early 1980s, reaching around 100 to 1 in the early 1990s and rising to 300–400 to 1 by the 2000s, although it has moderated a bit since then.

The 'owner's capitalism' of the past has been replaced by 'manager's capitalism' today that is only 'efficient' for the new class of professional managers who dominate the companies they now run but not so much for their businesses or for society in general. Today companies are so big that their managers can't afford to own much of them. They have less 'skin in the game' of the businesses they manage than their plutocratic predecessors did. Now if they fail they have multimillion-dollar severance packages ('golden parachutes'), 'golden umbrellas', options back-dating, deferred compensations schemes, and all kinds of gratui-tous payments above and beyond contractually agreed severance benefits, such as guaranteed consulting fees (often for virtually no work) and access to a dazzling range of expensive perks such as the use in retirement of corporate jets, chauffeured cars and exclusive club memberships to cushion the blow of failure.[31] When Stanley O'Neil resigned as the CEO of the US investment firm Merrill Lynch (as it was then known) in 2007 after it lost $8 billion, his severance package included company stock and options exceeding $160 million beyond the $90 million in total compensation he had earned as CEO the preceding year. The former CEO of Walt Disney, Michael Ovitz, left that position after just fifteen months with a severance package worth $38 million in cash and $100 million in company stock. This kind of thing is now so common we have a term for it: rewarding failure.

There is no obvious efficiency in making already extremely wealthy executives even wealthier, for example by paying billion-aire Tesla founder and CEO Elon Musk billions more dollars for one year's work, no matter how talented he may be.[32] This truism, called 'diminishing marginal utility' by economists, is known to every first-year economics undergraduate but not, apparently, to corporate boards of directors. Most of the wealth of such people is invested and adds little, if anything, to their already opulent lives or to the wider economy. Some of it gets spent on ostentatious displays of conspicuous consumption, such as $100 million paintings by famous artists which serve as status symbols for the super-rich and as a 'hedge against inflation' (as a consequence of which art galleries can now no longer afford to buy them), polluting super-yachts with their own onboard submarines and helicopters, and rockets to launch themselves into Earth's outer atmosphere. Spread more evenly across a wider range of people (like ordinary workers), this excess would be a great deal more 'efficient' at promoting general well-being.

The managers of large companies now effectively determine their own compensation, which helps to explain why it has reached such scandalous levels. Members of compensation committees of large corporations are typically other well-paid executives, retired executives and too-frequently friends and associates of those whose compensation they are setting. These committees now routinely employ 'compensation consultants' to advise them on executive pay, further ratcheting it up with hiring bonuses ('golden hellos') for managers they are looking to recruit. Bonuses now make up a majority of compensation packages of most senior executives, usually far exceeding their basic pay. This has led to a huge increase in wealth for these lucky few, both absolutely and relatively, with a negligible connection to the actual performance of their companies. There is mounting evidence that very little or no connection exists between CEO compensation and long-term stock performance. For example, a study of FTSE 350 companies by the University of Lancaster Management School concluded that only a 'negligible' link existed between executive pay and the performance of the firms it examined.[33] Some studies have even found a negative relationship between them. The corporate research firm MSCI compared the pay of about eight hundred American CEOs with shareholder returns for four hundred large and medium-sized US companies from 2006 and 2015. They found that they were inversely related; the firms with the lowest-paid CEOs outperformed those with the highest paid by nearly 39 per cent. 'Long term', it concluded, 'these findings suggest that the 40-year-old approach of using equity compensation to align the interests of CEOs with shareholders may be broken'.[34] The value of most shares is affected mainly by broad macroeconomic trends, like tracker funds, that have little, if anything, to do with the performance of particular managers. The market rises, carrying firms with it, and their managers are rewarded with absurdly generous bonuses. They are now usually rewarded with bonuses when the market falls too, albeit somewhat smaller. It is a system in which senior managers cannot lose, no matter what happens, which shows that it is a rigged game.

This is a global trend, although it is at its most extreme in the United States, leading to widespread disgust and cynicism about the justification for such rewards, and provoking a backlash against what many perceive as nothing more than rampant corporate greed by senior executives gaming the system for their own advantage. The Nobel laureate Paul Krugman has referred to it as 'the Great CEO Pay Heist'. In Switzerland a 2013 referendum on limiting executive pay and increasing the power of shareholders in corporate governance was passed by a majority of 67.9 per cent.

The Cambridge economist Ha-Joon Chang also notes that shareholders today are the most 'mobile' of stakeholders in a company, which is why they often care the least about its long-term future and so acquiesce to extravagant CEO compensation packages. Few shareholders are like Warren Buffett. They buy and sell shares regularly with relatively little commitment to the long-term value or viability of the firms they invest in. The CEOs focus increasingly on maximising the share price of the businesses they manage, which keeps most shareholders happy. And CEOs control the boardrooms through interlocking directorships and the manipulation of information. Boards of directors are often little more than 'Christmas tree decorations', who ask few questions and are told what chief executives want them to hear. The other gatekeepers of the system, such as auditors, regulators, credit rating agencies and market analysts, have also proved to be weak, compromised and ineffective, if not actually corrupt, as we saw in the financial crisis of 2008. This is a system that Nils Gilman appropriately calls 'plutonomy' – 'an economy geared to the interests of plutocrats'.[35]

The Anglo-Dutch writer Bernard Mandeville caused a scandal in 1714 with his book *The Fable of the Bees: or Private Vices, Publick Benefits*. In it, he claims that the traditional Christian idea of virtue based on self-sacrifice is really just a hypocritical mask for the self-interest that lies at the root of all human behaviour. This mask is unnecessary, he believes, because each of us pursuing our own selfish interests leads to general economic prosperity; private vices are public benefits.

Today, far from shocking opinion, the idea of 'private vices, public benefits' is an article of faith among mainstream economists and ideological proponents of laissez-faire capitalism. It is also the foundation of contemporary neoliberalism, which sees markets as more or less self-regulating, requiring only occasional correction; they function best for the public good when left alone (Capitalist Myth #4). This is the core of the 'market failure approach' that dominates thinking in most governments in the West and across most of the political spectrum now. It is the central dogma of the 'Washington Consensus'.

But what if Mandeville was wrong and the more or less free operation of markets tends to harm public welfare? What if private vices lead to public harm? Regulations are meant to be sufficient to curb the excesses of the free market and protect the public interest, but the crisis of 2008 proved the utter inadequacy of that assumption. While some piecemeal reforms have been introduced since then, very few bankers were tried for their part in a financial meltdown that almost brought the entire system down and cost millions of jobs and trillions of dollars. The system remains vulnerable to some of the same problems that existed before the crisis. For example, leverage can still be thirty times equity for banks.[36] And the problem of 'too-big-to-fail' remains. This partly explains the recent strength of both right-wing and left-wing populist movements which express a common perception that the public interest is not best served by this system and there is mounting anger at the failure of mainstream political parties to address it. Fewer people now believe that what is good for GM, or Amazon or Exxon, is good for America, or the world. It is self-evident that what is good for large multinational corporations is good for them and only them. That should be the starting assumption of any economic system that succeeds neoliberalism.

It is also apparent that what is in the interests of political parties is not necessarily in the interests of the people they govern, either. Most SOEs are owned by states dominated by one party or individual with little or no democratic account-ability. We should not assume that they will be any less self-interested than private businesses are. However, in more open societies in more democratic states there is at least a possibility that large corporations will act in the public interest if they are state owned. There is no such possibility in private hands. Something is better than nothing and, as Prince Faisal said in *Lawrence of Arabia*, 'no man needs nothing'.

7

THE STATE WE NEED

Much of modern political history has been a struggle, frequently bloody, over not just who controls states, but over their form and purposes too. For centuries writers have been sketching blueprints of the ideal state that politicians, statesmen and revolutionaries have tried to implement, sometimes violently. During the English Civil War, Thomas Hobbes made the case for an absolute state whose sole aim was to contain the conflict to which he believed humans are naturally prone. John Locke rejected Hobbes's arguments in favour of a limited constitutional state, as did the American founding fathers who were so strongly influenced by him. The American state was in large measure inspired by Locke's ideas and the revolution that they helped to inspire was essentially a war over two competing conceptions of the state. The French Revolutionaries turned to the Swiss writer Jean-Jacques Rousseau rather than Locke for their vision of a radically democratic state that would mould its members into public-spirited citizens. The Bolsheviks led by Vladimir Lenin would claim to be following Karl Marx's theories when they seized the teetering state in Russia in the name of the working class in October 1917. Mao Zedong did the same in 1949, albeit with 'Chinese characteristics'. There have also been fascist states, theocratic states, federal states and unitary states. In the world today there are almost two hundred sovereign, independent states whose varied forms span a broad range.

Despite the dreams of political philosophers, there really is no single, ideal form of the state. The most appropriate form depends on principles and circumstances, both of which vary from time to time and place to place. Principles guide us on the purposes of the state, but these are not universally shared. Circumstances tell us what is realistically achievable at any given moment and are therefore subject to change over time. So what type of state do we need now, and why?

What Are States For?

The answer to these questions depends on what we think the purpose of the state should be. In the circumstances in which we now find ourselves, in the aftermath of the financial crisis of 2008 and the Covid pandemic, the state we need has three basic purposes: security, welfare and democratic control of both politics and the economy.

What the philosopher Bernard Williams called the 'first political question', posed most powerfully by Hobbes almost four centuries ago, is how best to keep the people safe.[1] I have argued (in Chapter One) that this was the main preoccupation of the classical state of the early modern period in the West that emerged out of the disordered complexity of feudalism. States exist first and foremost to provide order and security for their citizens, to protect them from bodily harm and 'violent death', as Hobbes put it. Peace is prior to other goods since it is a precondition for them. A state that does not fulfil this basic purpose is a failed state. The power of some non-state actors today, such as drug cartels, pirates, terrorists, warring tribes, multinational corporations, international agencies and organised criminal gangs, has pushed some states to the brink of failure and beyond and caused others to lose control over some of their own territory, thereby preventing them from protecting the citizens there.

Most states in the world today face no such risk. Indeed, in general they tend to be very stable compared to states in the past. While the state has retreated in many spheres, its power and range have been extended in others, largely as a consequence of technological change. This is most obvious in its ability to monitor and control its own internal population. As more and more of our lives are conducted online the ability of states to snoop on us has increased dramatically. Threats of terrorism and online fraud have provided a pretext for peering into our online lives, where most of us spend increasing amounts of our time. The mass migration of data to the internet in recent decades has enabled states to track our digital footprints and create detailed profiles of their citizens' activities. Satellites, drones, CCTV cameras and other such devices have added to the arsenal of instruments at the disposal of states to monitor us. National security and intelligence agencies tend to err on the side of collecting more information than less, often indiscriminately vacuuming up enormous amounts of it. We now face the real prospect of a 'surveillance state' and, with it, a dramatic erosion of personal privacy, which may eventually disappear entirely when there's no place left to hide from the incessant surveillance of our lives.

These same technologies that have done so much to empower states are also available to private corporations, which are just as greedy to track us as states are. It enables them to target their advertising with greater precision and sell user data to third parties. They use cookies to track the websites you visit via your web browser and they have access to your private data on your smartphone apps and other devices. Just one company, Facebook, has 2.5 billion active monthly users with significant amounts of personal information on all of them, more than the population of any country. Businesses also now routinely employ surveillance technologies in the workplace to observe their staff, including keylogger computer software, video cameras, geolocation software and tracking website access and social media activity. All large and powerful agencies, whether private or public, are the beneficiaries of technological improvement. If anything, they may have become too powerful today in the areas that the early classical state found so difficult to police because it lacked the means to do so effectively.

The welfare state that first began to emerge in the West in the late nineteenth century and really took off after World War Two expressed a much broader and more ambitious idea of what states are for than the classical state that preceded it. The state came to be seen as existing not merely to protect its citizens from physical harm but also to promote their general well-being through the provision of basic human goods that we are all presumed to need, such as health, welfare and education. This new state did not replace the classical state, since it still sought to keep the peace. But it added a major new purpose to the goal of security, one that rapidly expanding industrial economies in the West were increasingly able to fund. This was a radical change that led to a vast expansion in the power and activity of states, in the process greatly improving the lives of millions through increased access to free healthcare and public education and fundamentally altering the relationship between states and their citizens.

The postwar welfare state expanded greatly in the decades leading up to the 1970s, when its limits appeared to have been reached, at least in the opinion of a growing body of politicians, economists and intellectuals. Gradually, what is known today as 'neoliberalism' became dominant and profoundly altered public policy across the political and ideological spectrum and around much of the world. The balance shifted away from states towards markets, which governments increasingly saw as the solution to the problems that afflicted bloated, inefficient states. The neoliberal state sees the purpose of government as more limited than the welfare state, favouring 'market solutions' in many areas that had recently been the responsibility of the state. An ambitious project to 'roll back the frontiers of the state' by selling off many of its assets and businesses, outsourcing some of its functions and deregulating much of the economy has not dismantled the welfare state, but has checked its growth and, in many cases, reversed it or diminished its capacity to provide for its citizens.

For a generation now defenders of the welfare state have fought against relentless political and ideological pressure to replace it with the more market-friendly neoliberal state. I have shown here some of the most damaging effects that this attempted revolution has had on the provision of basic goods and the extent to which it has benefited private corporations at the expense of the public interest. This is not the state we need now. It has been tried and has failed too many people who rely on the state for a great deal more than the neoliberal state is prepared to provide. I have shown why neoliberalism's naïve faith in the purported blessings of free markets is dangerously misplaced, which explains its practical failure, the most obvious and damaging example of which occurred in the financial crisis of 2008. In speaking of the 'return of the state' I mean to refer to the return of the state that provides these essential public goods to all of its citizens; a rolling back of the roll-back of the state, you might say. It would be a return to the social democratic welfare state in which all citizens are provided with key public goods and services fully and properly funded through taxation and, when necessary, printing money. And it would be a state we engage with as democratic citizens rather than as consumers or clients, a state that expresses the popular will to the extent that is practically possible in the vast and complex states of today.

Probably the biggest change to the state since the neoliberal era began has been its steady withdrawal from active involvement in the economy except during periodic crises, when it has jumped in to rescue failing businesses or markets. But otherwise states have surrendered much of their role in the economy, which is now dominated by the increasingly unbounded new leviathans of big business. Previously, the state had been expected to intervene in capitalist markets to regulate them, curb their excesses, bail out their biggest failures, set and enforce standards that few businesses would meet voluntarily, and redistribute wealth by means of progressive taxation. While most states still do all of these things to some degree, they do much less of them now than in the past, at least in the West.

This has been a matter of deliberate policy. According to the logic of neoliberalism, freeing markets through widespread deregulation, privatisations, austerity and outsourcing is normal but taxpayer bailouts are sometimes necessary to correct occasional market excesses.

The financial crisis of 2008 was a crisis of neoliberalism and may actually mark the beginning of its end. It is too early to tell. It laid bare the myths and delusions that underlie and justify its conception of the ideal balance between states and markets. As states stepped back from the market in the closing decades of the twentieth century and the opening years of the twenty-first, corporations expanded to fill the void. They were then gripped by an 'irrational exuberance', as Federal Reserve board chairman Alan Greenspan described it in 1996, while many states were in thrall to an ideology that bore little resemblance to the realities of how capitalist markets actually operate. When this system failed in 2008, neoliberal dogma was hastily dropped in the clamour for government bailouts. Virtually overnight the state became the solution to the defects of the market rather than the other way around, suddenly reversing the 'logic' of neoliberalism. However, it was not long before things returned to 'business as usual' and states again retreated from markets as quickly as they could. Initial promises of root-and-branch reform were followed by token gestures, half measures and cosmetic improvements. Capitalism had survived yet another crisis and neoliberalism has resumed its position as the dominant ideology, at least in the West. But faith in markets was very badly, perhaps irreversibly, shaken, even if government policies rarely reflect it. And things have been moving in a different direction beyond the West, particularly in East Asia and South America, where scepticism about neoliberalism is widespread and growing.

The crisis of 2008 has boosted confidence in the state for its critical role in saving the financial system from complete collapse. The Coronavirus pandemic that began in 2020 reinforced this confidence, even if it has not been universally recognised or appreciated. British prime minister Boris Johnson credited the success of his country's mass vaccination scheme operated and funded by his own government to private business. 'The reason we have the vaccine success', he declared to astonished cabinet colleagues, 'is because of capitalism, because of greed my friends', a reference to the fact that it was manufactured by the UK-based pharmaceutical giant AstraZeneca, even though the vaccine was almost entirely funded by taxpayers and charitable trusts.[2]

It has become increasingly obvious that the neoliberal experiment has failed and that a new understanding of states and markets is needed to replace it. The state needs to return to a more direct, active role in the economy as the agent of the public interest and as a check on the vast and expanding power of private corporations.

A policy of 'publicisation' (a better term for what is usually called 'nationalisation', which comes with too much baggage) would reverse the policies of privatisation and outsourcing that have transferred so many of the functions of the state to the market in recent decades. Industries could be taken into public ownership, particularly in sectors of the economy that produce important public goods and provide essential services that everyone should have access to. State-owned enterprises could redirect profits from private shareholders and overpaid managers to governments to support public purposes and advance shared goals. Natural monopolies such as water, electricity, oil and gas, roads and transportation would be obvious candidates for publicisation. Even if some of these publicised industries lose money, as enthusiasts for privatisation will insist is almost certain, they should still be subsidised by governments in cases where there is a strong public interest in doing so, and where it would sustain whole communities that are dependent on it. State-owned enterprises should not have profit maximisation as their sole purpose anyway. Indeed, it is one of their greatest advantages that they do not. Neither the British Broadcasting Corporation nor the Canadian Broadcasting Corporation, both publicly funded, seeks to make a 'profit' in monetary terms. Nor should they be expected to, any more than schools or hospitals should. They exist to provide important public goods.

Banks must be a central part of this process. This was apparent long before the financial crisis of 2008, although that disaster should have convinced all but the most fanatical market fundamentalists. Over two and a half centuries ago the Scottish economist Adam Smith warned about the 'particular orders of men who tyrannise the government'. He was referring primarily to commercial interests. Any major institutions crucial to the economic life of a democracy that are 'too big to fail' are in a strong position to be tyrannical in just this way. And, if they are big enough, then they are effectively public institutions anyway since they are guaranteed by the taxpayers, despite paying profits to their private shareholders, the worst possible combination for the general public. The banks that were bailed out in 2008 because of their own recklessness should have become state-owned enterprises permanently when they agreed to be saved by taxpayers. Instead, most were returned to private ownership. So the cycle begins all over again.

Publicly owned banks today may be relatively rare, but they do exist. In 1969 the Indian government nationalised fourteen of the country's largest private banks and added another six in 1980. The Mexican government nationalised its entire banking system in 1982 following a debt crisis and the Israeli government took ownership of four of the nation's largest banks in 1983. Many governments bailed out private banks that faced collapse in the years leading to the financial meltdown of 2008. These institutions found themselves drowning in a sea of bad debt when the US subprime mortgage market imploded. The UK government acquired 100 per cent of both Bradford and Bingley and Northern Rock banks, most of the shares in the Royal Bank of Scotland, and a substantial portion of

HBOS-Lloyds-TSB. When the American bank Citigroup became insolvent the US government bailed it out with a massive loan and took a 36 per cent equity stake in the company, which it unfortunately soon sold. The crisis also led to the nationalisation of the entire Icelandic banking industry and to a majority of the Irish banking sector and banks in Latvia, the Netherlands and Portugal. In most cases these banks were later reprivatised. Although neoliberal theory allows for temporary nationalisation in extreme cases, this cycle is likely to continue until it is finally broken, and the best way to do that is with permanent public ownership, as in India today.

The public appetite for publicisation is now strong after decades of neoliberal failure. In Britain, a 2017 poll by the Legatum Institute and Populus found overwhelming support for publicly owned water (83 per cent), electricity and gas (77 per cent), railways (76 per cent) and defence and aerospace industries (66 per cent). Opinion was evenly divided on banks (50/50).[3] A YouGov poll the same year found that majorities preferred state ownership of the postal service (65 per cent), railways (60 per cent), water (59 per cent) and energy (53 per cent). Half of Britons favoured public ownership of bus companies (50 per cent), although just 28 per cent in this poll supported it for banks. The same poll conducted by YouGov in 2019 registered increased support for nationalising all of these industries: the postal service (69 per cent), railways (64 per cent), water (63 per cent), buses (55 per cent) and energy (52 per cent).[4]

These results are consistent with growing public support for greater general government intervention in the economy, particularly to protect the environment.[5] In a YouGov poll in 2016 more people in Britain viewed capitalism unfavourably (39 per cent) than socialism unfavourably (32 per cent). Conversely, more had a favourable opinion of socialism (36 per cent) than of capitalism (33 per cent).[6]

Much depends here on what is meant by 'socialism' and 'capitalism'. Both take many forms. The form of capitalism that most people in the West know personally today is neoliberal, which in practice means the dominance of private oligopolies. When, over four decades ago, Margaret Thatcher launched her 'crusade' for 'popular capitalism' that would 'spread the nation's wealth' and 'return power to the people' by creating a 'property-owning democracy' (all her own terms), no one knew just how far short of these promises it would fall. The economist Milton Friedman, one of the saints of the neoliberal church, said that 'one of the greatest mistakes is to judge policies and programs by their intentions rather than their results'. The most obvious result of the neoliberal experiment is that its main beneficiaries, perhaps the only beneficiaries, have been the 'one per cent', and the '0.1 per cent' even more so, not ordinary people.

This may explain why the young are among the most receptive now to alternatives. A 2021 poll for the Institute of Economic Affairs found substantial support for 'millennial socialism' in the UK among people aged sixteen to thirty-four;

of these, 67 per cent would like to live in a socialist economic system.[7] Even in the United States a 2019 Gallup poll found that 43 per cent of Americans believe that socialism would be a good thing for the country, versus 51 per cent against (among Democrats socialism was viewed positively by 57 per cent). The same polls in 1942 found only 25 per cent affirming socialism as a good thing.[8] A Pew poll found 42 per cent positive for socialism and 55 per cent negative.[9]

I am not advocating socialism, if by that is meant full collective or state ownership of the means of production (factories, equipment, natural resources, capital, land). I am advocating a final end to the neoliberalism experiment and a radical shift in the balance between public and private power from the latter to the former. As the main expression of public power in the world today, the state should have a much greater involvement in economic life, which will otherwise be wholly dominated by markets, themselves under the controlling hegemony of a small number of unaccountable multinational mega-corporations.

All economies are mixed. In reality, there is no pure capitalism or pure socialism. So what is the best mix? We now know that the answer is *not* neoliberalism, unless you are a wealthy plutocrat. And even they are only neoliberals until their businesses need to be bailed out; you will struggle to find many neoliberals in corporate boardrooms then. The best mix is one in which the public interest is always paramount and where the economy is substantially, although not completely, within the sphere of democratic accountability, if not directly, then via governments elected by voters. Such a 'Public Interest State', as I call it, is one in which the economy serves public purposes rather than the other way around. While regulation of private businesses will always be necessary as long as they exist, it is not sufficient. Public ownership should play a much more substantial part in economic life than it has under neoliberalism if the public good is to count for as much as it should.

The Public Interest State

The state we need must be stronger, richer and bigger than the neoliberal state it replaces, since it must be able to check the enormous and growing power of private multinational corporations. But size and strength, while necessary, are not sufficient. It must also act primarily for the common good. While this does not necessarily mean it has to be a democratic state, since authoritarian states are capable of acting in the public interest, it is preferable that it is democratic, since then it would ultimately be accountable to its citizens. What I call the Public Interest State would bring much more of the economy under greater democratic control, which means a significant expansion of the state's role in economic life than allowed for by neoliberal ideology. The market and the state are forms of power, but one always and necessarily seeks profit and serves corporate interests, while the other can, and at least some of the time does, serve the public interest. This basic truth should be the starting point of any discussion about the role of the state today.

States come in many forms, only some of which are democratic. Whatever their defects, democracies have the great advantage of empowering their citizens to regularly hold their representatives to account for their actions at the ballot box. This gives public power in a democratic state a special responsibility for promoting and protecting the common good since it is meant to express the popular will. There is no such responsibility in private corporations, which largely operate in secret and are answerable to their shareholders, at least in principle. As consumers we can sometimes choose not to buy from them, but as citizens we should expect them to act in their own selfish interests within the bounds of the law, rather than in the public interest. Public interest is the duty of the state. In practice this expectation is honoured more in the breach than in the observance, I grant, but it is still an obligation of states that is sometimes realised. A central contention of this book is that democratic states in the West have too often failed to meet this obligation that has long been one of the central purposes of the state and, in my view, should remain so.

Outside the West, in the developing world, public and private power are, in general, more evenly balanced, although in some places, such as China, public power is paramount. But many of these states are not democratic, so their political leaders cannot be held to account for their policies any more than private corporations can. They would benefit by extending democracy, just as Western states would benefit from greater public power and an enlargement of our view of what the state can and should do.

Democracy ought to be applied to the economy as well as to politics to allow greater participation by workers, consumers and ordinary citizens in the economic decisions that affect their lives, both in public and private corporations. Economic democracy covers a broad range of policies that vary in their radicalism, from more participative management methods to fanciful utopian schemes without states, money or markets. They should all be part of a public debate about the transition to a post-neoliberal world.

For example, the practice of 'codetermination', where workers are directly involved in the internal management of the companies that employ them, has been government policy in some European countries, such as Norway, Sweden and Germany, for many years. It involves giving employees seats (usually 20 to 40 per cent) on their company's board of directors so that they have a formal role in its governance. Typically they are voted on to the board by their fellow workers. Codetermination may also include work councils whose representatives have rights of information, consultation and decision-making over working conditions in the company. In countries where codetermination has long been practised in industry it enjoys broad support and is not regarded as radical, even by most employers. That's because it isn't. It is a moderate and sensible form of shared governance that gives employees an important role in the economic decisions that immediately affect them. It should be the norm rather than the exception.

Given the importance that central banks and large financial institutions play in the economic life of nations today, their boards of directors should include citizen and employee representation as well. While this proposal would alarm economists and technocrats, who typically believe that politics should be kept out of economics as a realm for experts only, economics *is* political since it involves power. And in a democracy power should be in the hands of the people.

This argument for greater democratic involvement in politics and economics is only as effective as our democracy, which isn't very. Liberal democracy as it is practised in the West today is a very limited form of democracy. Some say it is no democracy at all. It has political parties, elections and a free press, but the public is mostly apathetic about politics and in practice democracy today has many oligarchic features. According to the political scientist Colin Crouch, Western capitalist societies are rapidly heading towards a system of 'post-democracy' whose outer 'formal shell' is democratic but whose inner workings are dominated by a wealthy elite.[10] As we have seen, the neoliberal policies that I have outlined here have removed much of the economy from the domain of democratic politics through privatisation, outsourcing and deregulation. Restoring it to that domain would help to revitalise democracy, although the practical limits on this in a massive, complex political and economic system of the kind we currently inhabit are considerable.

Nor is democracy a guarantee against abuse. Empowering the state is dangerous, no matter what form it takes. Strong states, including strong democratic states, can oppress people, foment wars and even conscript their citizens to fight. But disempowering the state is also dangerous, since it strengthens corporate power, which can also be tyrannical. And to do any good in the world requires power. Promoting public health, reducing suffering, increasing prosperity and preserving peace would all be impossible without power. Both strong states and weak states are risky in their own ways. The very same power that can do good can do bad. For example, discoveries in biology have led to life-saving medicines while also enabling us to create deadly biological weapons.

Power is not in itself good or bad. What is good and bad are the uses that are made of it, and that ultimately depends on the people in whose hands it resides. The English philosopher John Stuart Mill was right that 'the worth of a State, in the long run, is the worth of the individuals composing it'. A polity whose citizens have no sense of common political identity and don't care about the public good or the well-being of others is unlikely to use the power it has for those ends. Their inclination to do so is ultimately a matter of 'habits of the heart', of norms and values and how deeply and effectively they are ingrained in a population, more than formal laws and institutions. It is notoriously difficult to influence such things. Political thinkers since Plato have speculated on how best to instil such public spiritedness. We should not expect any simple institutional magic bullet will once and for all relieve us of the need to cultivate concern for the common good, which is a never-ending obligation. A strong state is necessary today to champion the public interest in a world increasingly dominated by overbearing forms of private power, but it is not sufficient. An equally strong commitment to the common good is also necessary to move the state in the right direction. Only a Public Interest State offers protection from the predations of unaccountable corporate power.

CONCLUSION

The state has been cast as the chief villain in the ideology of neoliberalism that has dominated our politics and economics for a generation now. It is usually depicted as inefficient, bureaucratic, and an impediment to general prosperity compared to free markets. Restrictions imposed to contain the spread of the Covid-19 virus have provoked even angrier hostility from some quarters, with talk of a 'police state' and 'totalitarianism' by many of the same people who had earlier warned about the dangers of the 'Deep State' – a shadowy cabal of self-appointed and unaccountable defenders of the permanent interests of the state among senior military commanders, civil servants and the security services. This was a major theme of the 2016 US presidential election and is an important element of the populist image of the state that Donald Trump and others have used to great political effect. We heard relatively little about the 'Deep State' during the US election in 2020, perhaps because Trump had surrounded himself in office with so many former generals, Bush-era appointees, Goldman Sachs alumni, corporate lawyers, bankers and multimillionaires that any mention of a 'Deep State' would likely only cause him Deep Embarrassment, if he was capable of that. But fears about state power persist and are by no means confined to American libertarians. Covid-19 restrictions have provoked protests, strikes and even riots in India, Belgium, the US, Britain, Germany, France, the Netherlands, Australia, Canada, Argentina and other places.

In political debate today one side typically rails only against the dangers of state power while the other usually sounds the alarm only about the hazards of corporate power. Both are right to some degree. It is impossible accurately to assess public power in abstraction from private power, the state in isolation from the market. The benefits and risks that one presents can only be understood relative to the other, which is why I have devoted so much attention here to non-state powers. The case for the state depends to a large extent on the strength and nature of private forms of power. The key question is what balance there should be between public and private power.

But, in general today, the risks of private power are too often understated or even ignored, and the benefits of public power too little appreciated. The balance between them in the West now favours private power too much; the pendulum has swung too far towards the market. This has led to many damaging pathologies and iniquities and has too often allowed private interests to dominate the public interest. It has also deformed our conception of what states are for and how we relate to them, which should be as citizens rather than as consumers. Misled by fashionable ideologies, our leaders have done a poor job of judging this matter, and thereby undermined many important public goods and blighted lives in the process.

We now live in a world of big – big businesses, big states, big populations, big economies and big science. The scale of the human world has grown to often inhuman dimensions, which has made it seem as though the natural world is shrinking. In many respects it is, literally, in the forests of the Amazon, the ice caps of the Arctic and the coral reefs of Australia. Much as we might want to go back to a smaller, simpler, more 'human scale' world, for now that is not a realistic possibility. Neither is the primitive, emergent capitalism of the late eighteenth and early nineteenth centuries that Alexis de Tocqueville observed in small-town New England, so much admired today by the 'limited government' believers in civil society. Nor is the unregulated industrial capitalism of 1850s Britain that Karl Marx devoted his life to studying, so much admired today by free market libertarians. We cannot just pick and choose the form of capitalism we prefer, as if ordering from an à la carte menu. 'Men make their own history', Marx wisely cautioned, 'but they do not make it as they please; they do not make it under self-selected circumstances, but under circumstances existing already, given and transmitted from the past.'

Our capitalism is dominated by big, oligopolistic corporations, and likely will be for some time to come. That's why *our* state needs to be a Public Interest State, big and strong enough to provide and protect the most essential public goods for everyone in such a world. We know that states are capable of doing this, even if they often fail or fall well short. There is simply no way to guarantee that they will always act positively. But they are nonetheless our best hope today for maximising freedom and well-being for as many people as possible.

The early classical state was meant to protect us from physical violence and safeguard private property. The welfare state promised to provide a range of freedom-enhancing and life-enriching goods to all citizens that free markets never did and likely never would. The neoliberal state has retreated from these provisions without entirely abandoning them. And it has greatly enhanced the freedom and power of private business, leaving most of us exposed to economic harm from these corporate behemoths. The state must protect us from such harm no less than it protects us from physical harm.

States and markets periodically change, sometimes radically, and so does the relationship between them. Attitudes to them change too. It is now possible to perceive signs of change in all of these ways. How far this change will go remains unclear. What is clear is that it needs to go far. We require strong states to counter strong corporations and to promote and protect the public interest. Nothing else is capable of doing so today. As long as such private power exists, we need comparable, or even greater, public power to control it. The Public Interest State is now the only institution that might effectively check the growing dominance of corporate oligopolies and guarantee universal access to the most important human goods.

ENDNOTES

INTRODUCTION

1. Global Justice Now, '69 of the Richest 100 Entities on the Planet are Corporations, not Governments, Figures Show', www.globaljustice.org.uk, 17 October 2018. According to Global Justice Now, which compiled this list, 'these figures have been taken from a direct comparison of the annual revenue of corporations and the annual revenue of countries. Sources: CIA World Factbook 2017 and Fortune Global 500'.
2. Karl Marx and Friedrich Engels, *Manifesto of the Communist Party*, in *The Marx–Engels Reader*, 475.
3. Ian Bremmer, *The End of the Free Market: Who Wins the War Between States and Corporations* (London and New York: Portfolio, 2010), 5.
4. Joshua Kurlantzick, *State Capitalism: How the Return of Statism is Transforming the World* (Oxford: Oxford University Press, 2016), 4.
5. Bremmer, *End of the Free Market*, 20.
6. Ibid., 168.
7. Globe Scan, 'Economic System Seen as Unfair: Global Poll', www.globescan.com, 12 March 2012.

1 BUILDING A PEOPLE'S STATE

1. Martin van Creveld, *The Rise and Decline of the State* (Cambridge: Cambridge University Press, 1999), 57.
2. Andrew Vincent, *Theories of the State* (Oxford: Basil Blackwell, 1987), 29.
3. Ibid., 218.
4. Van Creveld, *Rise and Decline of the State*, 242.

5. Bernard Williams, *In the Beginning Was the Deed: Realism and Moralism in Political Argument* (Princeton and Oxford: Princeton University Press, 2005), 3.
6. Lord Hugh Cecil, *Conservatism* (London: Williams and Norgate, 1912), 170.
7. Mandy Smithberger, 'Brass Parachutes: The Problem of the Pentagon Revolving Door', www.pogo.org, 5 November 2018.
8. Daniel Cebul, 'New watchdog report decries "revolving door" between the Pentagon and defense contractors', www.defensenews.com, 6 November 2018.
9. Andrew Grice, '£850bn: official cost of the bank bailout', www.independent.co.uk, 4 December 2009.
10. First published in the *New-York Daily Tribune*, no. 4145, 1 August 1854 as a leader. http://marxengels.public-archive.net/en/ME1912en.html.
11. Max Roser and Esteban Ortiz-Ospina, 'Literacy', https://ourworldindata.org, last revision 20 September 2018.
12. Andrew Cumbers, *Reclaiming Public Ownership: Making Space for Economic Democracy* (London and New York: Zed Books, 2012), 14.
13. Paul Cohen, 'Lessons from the Nationalization-Nation: State-Owned Enterprises in France', *Dissent* 57, no. 1 (2010), 16.
14. Peter Hall, *Governing the Economy: The Politics of State Intervention in Britain and France* (Cambridge: Polity Press, 1986), 153.
15. Cohen, 'Lessons from the Nationalization-Nation', 19.
16. Carlos Aguiar de Medeiros, 'Asset-Stripping the State', *New Left Review*, 55 (2009), 112–13. The comparison did not include the US, where the figure exceeded 16.5 per cent; nor of course the Soviet Union or China.

2 PRIVATE GOOD, PUBLIC BAD

1. Friedrich Hayek, *The Constitution of Liberty* (London: Routledge, 2006).
2. James Meek, *Private Island: Why Britain Now Belongs to Someone Else* (London and New York: Verso, 2014), 8.
3. Rupert Jones, 'Home ownership in England at a 30-year low, official figures show', www.theguardian.com, 2 March 2007.
4. Meek, *Private Island*, 15.
5. Andrew Cumbers, 'Renewing Public Ownership: Constructing a Democratic Economy in the Twenty-First Century', https://classonline.org.uk, 10 October 2017.
6. Carlos Aguiar de Medeiros, 'Asset-Stripping the State', *New Left Review*, 109–10.
7. Janine R. Wedel, 'The Harvard Boys Do Russia', www.thenation.com, 14 May 1998.
8. Tim Büthe and Walter Mattli, *The New Global Rulers: The Privatization of Regulation in the World Economy* (Princeton and Oxford: Princeton University Press, 2011), 5.
9. OECD Data, 'General Government Spending', https://data.oecd.org (accessed 12 December 2021).
10. Damien Cahill and Martijn Konings, *Neoliberalism* (Cambridge: Polity Press, 2017), 37–8.

11. OECD Data, 'General Government Spending'.
12. Margaret Thatcher, 'Leader's speech, Bournemouth 1986', www. britishpoliticalspeech.org (accessed 12 December 2021).
13. Tom Sasse et al., 'Government outsourcing: What has worked and what needs reform?' www.instituteforgovernment.org.uk, September 2019.
14. Ibid.
15. Peter J. Walker, 'Private firms earn £500m from disability benefit assessments', www.theguardian.com, 27 December 2016.
16. Robert Booth and Nick Hopkins, 'Olympic security chaos: depth of G4S security crisis revealed', www.theguardian.com, 13 July 2012.
17. Patrick Butler, 'Disabled people's "fit for work" assessments should be scrapped – MPs', www.theguardian.com, 23 July 2014.
18. Sasse et al., 'Government outsourcing'.
19. Congressional Research Service, 'Federal Workforce Statistics Sources: OPM and OMB', https://sgp.fas.org, updated 24 June 2021.
20. Chiara Cordelli, *The Privatized State* (Princeton and Oxford: Princeton University Press, 2020), 3.
21. Paul Verkuil, *Outsourcing Sovereignty: Why Privatization of Government Functions Threatens Democracy and What We Can Do About It* (Cambridge: Cambridge University Press, 2007), 26.

3 THE RISE OF PRIVATE GOVERNMENTS

1. Tom Wainwright, *Narconomics: How to Run a Drug Cartel* (New York: Public Affairs, 2016), 16.
2. David Korten, *When Corporations Rule the World*, 20th anniversary edition (Oakland: Berrett-Koehler, 2015), 76.
3. George Tindall Brown and David Shi, *America: A Narrative History*, vol. 2 (New York: W.W. Norton & Co., 2012), 589.
4. Steve Fraser, *The Age of Acquiescence: The Life and Death of American Resistance to Organized Wealth and Power* (New York: Little, Brown and Co., 2015), 66.
5. Ha-Joon Chang, *23 Things They Don't Tell You About Capitalism* (London: Penguin, 2011), 12.
6. Alfred Chandler and Bruce Mazlish (eds), *Leviathans: Multinational Corporations and the New Global History* (Cambridge: Cambridge University Press, 2005), 232.
7. Manfred Steger and Ravi Roy, *Neoliberalism: A Very Short Introduction* (Oxford: Oxford University Press, 2020), 7.
8. Oliver Bullough, *Moneyland: Why Thieves and Crooks Now Rule the World and How to Take It Back* (London: Profile Books, 2019), 31.
9. Damien Cahill and Martijn Konings, *Neoliberalism* (Cambridge: Polity Press, 2017), 97.
10. Chandler and Mazlish, *Leviathans*, 220.
11. Korten, *When Corporations Rule the World*, 26.
12. Jonathan Tepper, *The Myth of Capitalism: Monopolies and the Death of Capitalism* (Hoboken: Wiley, 2019), 11–12.

13. Cahill and Konings, *Neoliberalism*, 100.
14. Tepper, *The Myth of Capitalism*, 103.
15. Ibid., 23.
16. John Gerard Ruggie, 'Multinationals as global institution: Power, authority and relative autonomy', *Regulation & Governance*, 12 (2018), 320.
17. Bullough, *Moneyland*, 19.
18. Paul Kennedy, *Vampire Capitalism: Fractured Societies and Alternative Futures* (London: Palgrave Macmillan, 2017), 92.
19. Chandler and Mazlish, *Leviathans*, 8.
20. Jeremy Waddington, 'Trade union membership in Europe: The extent of the problem and the range of trade union responses', ETUI-REHS, www.fes.de, 1–2 July 2005.
21. United Nations and the Rule of Law, 'Sustainable Development Goal 16', www.un.org (accessed 12 December 2021).
22. Milton Friedman, *Capitalism and Freedom* (Chicago: University of Chicago Press, 2020), 133.
23. Joel Bakan, *The New Corporation: How 'Good' Corporations are Bad for Democracy* (New York: Vintage Books, 2020), 12.
24. Certified B Corporation, https://bcorporation.net (accessed 12 December 2021).
25. Bakan, *The New Corporation*, 19.
26. Ibid., 41.
27. Ibid., 16.
28. Lauren Feiner, 'Google cut its lobbying spending nearly in half in 2019, while Facebook took the lead', www.cnbc.com, 22 January 2020.
29. Bakan, *The New Corporation*, 26.
30. Drew Desilver, 'Despite global concerns about democracy, more than half of countries are democratic, www.pewresearch.org, 14 May 2019.
31. Anthony Cormier et al., 'The Untold Story of What Really Happened After HSBC, El Chapo's Bank, Promised to Get Clean', www.buzzfeednews.com, 21 September 2020.

4 PREYING ON THE WEAK

1. Hector Tobar, 'Ranking security official slain in Mexico', www.latimes.com, 9 May 2008.
2. Klaus von Lampe, *Organized Crime: Analyzing Illegal Activities, Criminal Structures, and Extra-Legal Governance* (London: Sage, 2016), 285.
3. Nicholas Barnes, 'Criminal Politics: An Integrated Approach to the Study of Organized Crime, Politics, and Violence', *American Political Science Review*, 15, no. 4 (2017), 969.
4. Ioan Grillo, *El Narco: The Bloody Rise of Mexican Drug Cartels* (London: Bloomsbury, 2012), 5.
5. Ibid., 206.
6. *Forbes* magazine, '#67 Joaquin Guzman Loera: Drug Trafficker, Sinaloa Cartel', www.forbes.com (accessed 12 December 2021).

7. CNN Editorial Research, 'Mexico Drug War Fast Facts', https://edition.cnn.com, updated 12 April 2021.
8. Global Financial Integrity, 'Executive Summary', www.gfintegrity.org/wp-content/uploads/2017/03/Transnational_Crime-final-_exec-summary.pdf (accessed 12 December 2021).
9. Grillo, *El Narco*, 147.
10. Reuters et al., 'Dutch police arrest alleged Asian drug syndicate kingpin', www.reuters.com, 24 January 2021.
11. Von Lampe, *Organized Crime*, 286.
12. Barnes, 'Criminal Politics', 977.
13. Mark Galeotti, 'Gangster's paradise: how organised crime took over Russia', www.theguardian.com, 23 March 2018.
14. Ibid.
15. Grillo, *El Narco*, 149.
16. Joseph Stiglitz, *Globalization and Its Discontents* (London and New York: Allen Lane, 2002), 150.
17. Anthony Galano III, 'International Monetary Fund Response to the Brazilian Debt Crisis: Whether the Effects of Conditionality Have Undermined Brazil's National Sovereignty?', *Pace International Law Review*, 6, no. 2 (1994), 340.
18. Stiglitz, *Globalization and Its Discontents*, 24.
19. Ben Clift, *The IMF and the Politics of Austerity in the Wake of the Global Financial Crisis* (Oxford: Oxford University Press).

5 WISHFUL THINKING BETWEEN STATE AND MARKET

1. Fred Powell, *The Politics of Civil Society: Big Society and Small Government* (Bristol: Policy Press, 2013), 3.
2. Alexis de Tocqueville, *Democracy in America*, ed. R. Heffner (New York: Mentor Books, 1956), 198.
3. Ibid., 202.
4. Phillip Blond, *Red Tory: How Left and Right Have Broken Britain and How We Can Fix It* (London: Faber and Faber, 2010), 63.
5. Ibid., 71.
6. Ibid., 153.
7. Roger Scruton, *Conservatism* (London: Profile Books, 2017), 35.
8. Ibid., 131.
9. Ibid., 131.
10. Patrick Deneen, *Why Liberalism Failed* (New Haven and London: Yale University Press, 2018), 61.
11. Ibid., 193.
12. Powell, *The Politics of Civil Society*, 148.
13. Noam Chomsky, 'Government in the Future', talk delivered at the Poetry Center, New York, 16 February 1970, https://www.youtube.com/watch?v=JmbLXlmlL4&list=PLslBB7Ebx4M6z2mEfLYgfmcGK-mgI94xr&index=32.
14. Noam Chomsky interviewed in Leiden, 14 March 2011, https://www.youtube.com/watch?v=60z2zGbGbfE&list=PLC33823D316D01309&index=3.

15. John Dewey, *The Later Works, 1925–1953*, vol. 6: *1931–32: Essays, Reviews and Miscellany*, ed. Jo Ann Boydston (Cabondale: Southern Illinois University Press, 1985), 164.

16. Noam Chomsky interviewed by Reddit Blog, 12 March 2010, https://www.youtube.com/watch?v=PiqPCRtzOBw&list=PLslBB7Ebx4M6z2mEfL YgfmcGK-mgI94xr&index=15.

17. Ibid.

18. Powell, *The Politics of Civil Society*, 199.

19. Ibid., 207.

20. Darin Christensen and Jeremy M. Weinstein, 'Defunding Dissent: Restrictions on Aid to NGOs', https://muse.jhu.edu, April 2013.

21. Sheree Johnson, 'New Research Sheds Light on Daily Ad Exposures', https://sjinsights.net, 29 September 2014.

22. Ibid.

23. American Psychological Association, 'Television advertising leads to unhealthy habits in children', www.apa.org, 2004.

24. Letizia Alvino et al. 'Picking Your Brains: Where and How Neuroscience Tools Can Enhance Marketing Research', *Frontiers of Science*, vol. 14 (2020), 1–20, 2.

25. Daniel Kahneman, *Thinking Fast and Slow* (London: Penguin, 2012).

26. David Rieff, 'The False Dawn of Civil Society', *The Nation* (4 February 1999), 12.

27. Lisa Schmeiser, 'The Effect of Facebook's Social Media Silo on Itself and You', https://observer.com, 5 March 2017.

28. Fazida Karim, Azeezat A. Oyewande, Lamis F. Abdalla, Reem Chaudhry Ehsanullah and Safeera Khan, 'Social Media Use and Its Connection to Mental Health: A Systematic Review', *Cureus* 12, no. 6 (2020).

6 STATE CAPITALISM: FROM WASHINGTON TO BEIJING

1. Full Fact, 'Do the public want the railways renationalised?', https://fullfact. org, 14 June 2018.

2. Joshua Kurlantzick, *State Capitalism: How the Return of Statism is Transforming the World* (Oxford: Oxford University Press, 2016), 22.

3. Ibid., 22.

4. Brigitta Jakob, 'Performance in Strategic Sectors: A Comparison of Profitability and Efficiency of State-Owned Enterprises and Private Corporations', https://core.ac.uk, 2017.

5. Norwegian Petroleum, 'The government's revenues', www.norskpetroleum.no (accessed 12 December 2021).

6. Jasper Jolly, 'Norway's sovereign wealth fund gains more than £90bn during 2020', www.theguardian.com, 28 January 2021.

7. Reuters Staff, 'Russia to spend up to $5.5 billion a year from wealth fund to boost state investment – official', www.reuters.com, 21 June 2021.

8. SWFI, 'Top 100 Largest Sovereign Wealth Fund Rankings by Total Assets', www.swfinstitute.org (accessed 12 December 2021).

9. Kurlantzick, *State Capitalism*, 230–31.

10. Ian Bremmer, *The End of the Free Market: Who Wins the War Between States and Corporations* (London and New York: Portfolio, 2010), 168.
11. Korin Kane, 'Size and sectoral distribution of state-owned enterprises', www.oecd.org, 28 September 2017.
12. Zarmina Ali, 'The world's 100 largest banks, 2020', www.spglobal.com, 7 April 2020.
13. Tiago Nasser Appel, 'Just how capitalist is China?', www.scielo.br, December 2014.
14. Kurlantzick, *State Capitalism*, 100.
15. Ibid., 3.
16. Ibid., 92.
17. Kane, 'Size and sectoral distribution of state-owned enterprises'.
18. Ali, 'The world's 100 largest banks, 2020'.
19. Kurlantzick, *State Capitalism*, 232.
20. Ibid., 101.
21. Bremmer, *End of the Free Market*, 168.
22. Carlos Aguiar de Medeiros, 'Asset-Stripping the State', *New Left Review*, 55 (2009), 112–13.
23. Ibid., 113.
24. Ibid., 113.
25. Mariana Mazzucato, *The Entrepreneurial State: Debunking Public vs Private Sector Myths* (London: Penguin, 2018), 79.
26. Ibid., 202–3.
27. Ibid., 4.
28. Bremmer, *End of the Free Market*, 4–5.
29. Ibid., 151.
30. Natalie Sabadish and Lawrence Mishel, 'CEO pay and the top 1%: How executive compensation and financial-sector pay have fueled income inequality', www.epi.org, 2 May 2012.
31. Ha-Joon Chang, *23 Things They Don't Tell You About Capitalism* (London: Penguin, 2011), 16.
32. Jenny Chu et al., 'Compensation consultants lead to higher CEO pay', www.jbs.cam.ac.uk, 11 November 2014.
33. Rob Davies, ' "Negligible" link between executive pay and firm's performance, says study', www.theguardian.com, 27 December 2016.
34. MSCI, 'Out of Whack: U.S. CEO Pay and Long-term Investment Returns', https://www.msci.com/ceo-pay (accessed 12 December 2021).
35. Nils Gilman, 'The Twin Insurgency', *Political Economy & the State* 9, no. 6 (2014).
36. Thom Wetzer, Jure Jeric and Alexandra Zeitz, 'Ten years After the Financial Crisis: "We Are Safer, But Not As Safe As We Should and Could Be"', Oxford Law Faculty Blog, https://www.law.ox.ac.uk/business-law-blog/blog/2018/11/ten-years-after-financial-crisis-we-are-safer-not-safe-we-should-and, 15 November 2018.

7 THE STATE WE NEED

1. Bernard Williams, *In the Beginning Was the Deed: Realism and Moralism in Political Argument* (Princeton and Oxford: Princeton University Press, 2005), 3.
2. Michael Safi, 'Oxford/AstraZeneca Covid vaccine research "was 97% publicly funded"', www.theguardian.com, 15 April 2021.
3. Matthew Elliott and James Kanagasooriam, 'Public opinion in the post-Brexit era: Economic attitudes in modern Britain', https://lif.blob.core.windows.net, October 2017.
4. Jon Stone, 'Public support for nationalisation increased while Jeremy Corbyn was Labour leader, poll finds', www.independent.co.uk, 16 December 2019.
5. Matt McGrath, 'Climate change: Polls shows rising demand for government action', www.bbc.co.uk/news, 28 October 2021.
6. Will Dahlgreen, 'British people keener on socialism than capitalism', https://yougov.co.uk, 23 February 2016.
7. Politics.co.uk Staff, 'Majority of young Brits want a socialist economic system', www.politics.co.uk, 6 July 2021.
8. Mohamed Younis, 'Four in 10 Americans Embrace Some Form of Socialism', https://news.gallup.com, 20 May 2019.
9. Pew Research Center, 'In Their Own Words: Behind Americans' Views of "Socialism" and "Capitalism"', www.pewresearch.org, 7 October 2019.
10. Colin Crouch, *Coping with Post-Democracy* (London: Fabian Society, 2000).

BIBLIOGRAPHY

Aguiar de Medeiros, Carlos. 'Asset-Stripping the State'. *New Left Review* 55 (2009): 109–32

Alvino, Letizia, et al. 'Picking Your Brains: Where and How Neuroscience Tools Can Enhance Marketing Research'. *Frontiers of Science* 14 (2020): 1–20

Appel, Tiago Nasser. 'Just How Capitalist is China?'. *Brazilian Journal of Political Economy* 34, no. 4 (2014): 656–69

Babic, Milan, et al. 'States versus Corporations: Rethinking the Power of Business in International Relations'. *International Spectator* 52, no. 4 (2017): 20–43

—. 'Who is more powerful – states or corporations?'. *The Conversation*. 10 July 2018

Bakan, Joel. *The New Corporation: How 'Good' Corporations are Bad for Democracy*. New York: Vintage Books, 2020

Barnes, Nicholas. 'Criminal Politics: An Integrated Approach to the Study of Organized Crime, Politics, and Violence'. *American Political Science Review* 15, no. 4 (2017): 967–87

Barnet, Richard, and John Cavanaugh. *Global Dreams: Imperial Corporations and the New World Order*. New York: Touchstone, 1994

Blond, Phillip. *Red Tory: How Left and Right Have Broken Britain and How We Can Fix It*. London: Faber and Faber, 2010

Bogle, John. *The Battle for the Soul of Capitalism*. New Haven: Yale University Press, 2005

Boyd, Christopher. 'The Demise of State Legitimacy: Is Globalisation the Villain of the Piece?'. *Groundings* 2 (2008): 30–50

Boycko, Maxim, Andrei Shleifer and Robert Vishny. *Privatizing Russia*. Cambridge, MA: MIT Press, 1995

Bremmer, Ian. *The End of the Free Market: Who Wins the War Between States and Corporations*. London and New York: Portfolio, 2010

BIBLIOGRAPHY

Bullough, Oliver. *Moneyland: Why Thieves and Crooks Now Rule the World and How to Take It Back*. London: Profile Books, 2018

Büthe, Tim, and Walter Mattli. *The New Global Rulers: The Privatization of Regulation in the World Economy*. Princeton and Oxford: Princeton University Press, 2011

Cahill, Damien, and Martijn Konings. *Neoliberalism*. Cambridge: Polity Press, 2017

Calderón, Laura Y., Kimberly Heinle, Octavio Rodríguez Ferreira and David A. Shirk. *Organized Crime and Violence in Mexico*. San Diego: Justice in Mexico, 2019

Cassese, Sabino. 'The Rise and Decline of the Notion of State'. *International Political Science Review* 7, no. 2 (1986): 120–30

Cassidy, John. 'The Real Cost of the 2008 Financial Crisis'. *New Yorker*, 10 September 2018

Caufield, Catherine. *Masters of Illusion: The World Bank and the Poverty of Nations*. New York: Henry Holt, 1996

Cecil, Lord Hugh. *Conservatism*. London: Williams and Norgate, 1912

Chandler, A., and B. Mazlish (eds). *Leviathans: Multinational Corporations and the New Global History*. Cambridge: Cambridge University Press, 2005

Chang, Ha-Joon. *Bad Samaritans: The Guilty Secrets of Rich Nations & the Threat to Global Prosperity*. London: Random House Business Books, 2008

—. *23 Things They Don't Tell You About Capitalism*. London: Penguin, 2011

Chomsky, Noam. *Failed States: The Abuse of Power and the Assault on Democracy*. London: Penguin, 2007

Clift, Ben. *The IMF and the Politics of Austerity in the Wake of the Global Financial Crisis*. Oxford: Oxford University Press, 2018

Cohen, Nick. *What's Left? How Liberals Lost Their Way*. London: HarperCollins, 2007

Cohen, Paul. 'Lessons from the Nationalization-Nation: State-Owned Enterprises in France'. *Dissent* 57, no. 1 (2010): 15–20

Cohen, Stephen. *Modern Capitalist Planning: The French Model*. London: Weidenfeld and Nicolson, 1969

Collier, Paul. *The Future of Capitalism: Facing the New Anxieties*. London: Penguin, 2018

Cordelli, Chiara. *The Privatized State*. Princeton and Oxford: Princeton University Press, 2020

Crouch, Colin. *Coping with Post-Democracy*. London: Fabian Society, 2000

Cumbers, Andrew. *Reclaiming Public Ownership: Making Space for Economic Democracy*. London and New York: Zed Books, 2012

—. 'Renewing Public Ownership: Constructing a Democratic Economy in the Twenty-First Century'. Centre for Labour and Social Studies, 2014

Deneen, Patrick. *Why Liberalism Failed*. New Haven and London: Yale University Press, 2018

Dunleavy, Patrick, and Brendan O'Leary. *Theories of the State: The Politics of Liberal Democracy*. Basingstoke: Macmillan, 1987

Foster, John Bellamy. 'What is Monopoly Capital?'. *Monthly Review* 68, no. 8 (2018)

Foucault, Michel. *Discipline and Punish: The Birth of the Prison*, trans. Alan Sheridan. New York: Vintage Books, 1995

BIBLIOGRAPHY

Friedman, Milton. *Capitalism and Freedom*. Chicago: University of Chicago Press, 2020

Galano, Anthony. 'International Monetary Fund Response to the Brazilian Debt Crisis: Whether the Effects of Conditionality Have Undermined Brazil's National Sovereignty?'. *Pace International Law Review* 6, no. 2 (1994): 323–51

Galeotti, Mark. *The Vory: Russia's Super-Mafia*. New Haven and London: Yale University Press, 2018

Gilman, Nils. 'The Twin Insurgency'. *The American Interest* 9, no. 6 (2014)

Grayling, A. C. *The Good State: On the Principles of Democracy*. London: Oneworld, 2020

Grillo, Ioan. *El Narco: The Bloody Rise of Mexican Drug Cartels*. London: Bloomsbury, 2012

Hall, Peter. *Governing the Economy: The Politics of State Intervention in Britain and France*. Cambridge: Polity Press, 1986

Hanna, Thomas. *Our Common Wealth: The Return of Public Ownership in the United States*. Manchester: Manchester University Press, 2018

Hayek, Friedrich. *The Constitution of Liberty*. London: Routledge, 2006

Hennock, Ernest Peter. *The Origin of the Welfare State in England and Germany, 1850–1914: Social Policies Compared*. Cambridge: Cambridge University Press, 2007

Hobbes, Thomas. *Leviathan*, ed. C. B. Macpherson. Harmondsworth: Penguin, 1968

Hutton, Will. *The State We're In*. London: Jonathan Cape, 1995

Jakob, Brigitta. 'Performance in Strategic Sectors: A Comparison of Profitability and Efficiency of State-Owned Enterprise and Private Corporations'. *Park Place Economist* 25, no. 1 (2017): 9–20

Jessop, Bob. 'Redesigning the State, Reorienting State Power, and Rethinking the State'. In *Handbook of Politics: State and Society in Global Perspective*, ed. K. Leicht and C. Jenkins. New York: Springer, 2009

Kahn, Si, and Elizabeth Minnich. *The Fox in the Henhouse: How Privatization Threatens Democracy*. San Francisco: Berrett-Koehler, 2005

Kahneman, Daniel. *Thinking, Fast and Slow*. London: Penguin, 2012

Kennedy, Paul. *Vampire Capitalism: Fractured Societies and Alternative Futures*. London: Palgrave Macmillan, 2017

Korten, David. *When Corporations Rule the World*, 20th anniversary edition. Oakland: Berrett-Koehler, 2015

Kurlantzick, Joshua. *State Capitalism: How the Return of Statism is Transforming the World*. Oxford: Oxford University Press, 2016

Kwiatkowski, Grzegorz, and Pawel Augustynowicz. 'State-Owned Enterprises in the Global Economy – Analysis Based on Fortune Global 500 List', conference paper, Management, Knowledge and Learning: Joint International Conference, 27–9 May 2015

Lenin, Vladimir. *The Lenin Anthology*, ed. R. Tucker. New York and London: W. W. Norton and Co., 1975

Locke, Rachel. *Organized Crime, Conflict, and Fragility: A New Approach*. New York: International Peace Institute, 2012

Luttwak, Edward. *Turbo-Capitalism: Winners and Losers in the Global Economy*. London: Weidenfeld and Nicolson, 1998

Maconie, Stuart. *The Nanny State Made Me: A Story of Britain and How to Save It*. London: Ebury Press, 2020

Madra, Yahya, and Fikret Adaman. 'Public economics after neoliberalism: a Theoretical-historical perspective'. *European Journal of the History of Economic Thought* 17, no. 4 (2010): 1079–106

Marx, Karl. *The Marx–Engels Reader*, ed. R. Tucker. New York and London: W. W. Norton and Co., 1978

Masquelier, Charles. 'Theorising French neoliberalism: The technocratic elite, decentralised collective bargaining and France's "passive neoliberal revolution"'. *European Journal of Social Theory* 24, no. 1 (2021): 65–85

Mazzucato, Mariana. *The Entrepreneurial State: Debunking Public vs Private Sector Myths*. London: Penguin, 2018

Meek, James. *Private Island: Why Britain Now Belongs to Someone Else*. London and New York: Verso, 2014

Mermin, Jonathan. 'Television News and American Intervention in Somalia: The Myth of a Media-Driven Foreign Policy'. *Political Science Quarterly* 112 (1997): 385–403

Mitchell, William, and Thomas Fazi. *Reclaiming the State: A Progressive Vision of Sovereignty for a Post-Neoliberal World*. London: Pluto Press, 2017

Morris, Christopher. 'The State'. In *The Oxford Handbook of the History of Political Philosophy*, ed. G. Klosko. Oxford: Oxford University Press, 2011

Müller, Karel. 'The Civil Society–State Relationship in Contemporary Discourse: A Complementary Account from Giddens' Perspective'. *British Journal of Politics and International Relations* 8 (2006): 311–30

Piketty, Thomas. *Capital in the Twenty-First Century*. Cambridge, MA: Belknap Press, 2017

Powell, Fred. *The Politics of Civil Society: Big Society and Small Government*. Bristol: Policy Press, 2013

Putnam, Robert D. *Bowling Alone: The Collapse and Revival of American Community*. New York and London: Simon & Schuster, 2000

Raineri, Luca, and Francesco Strazzari. 'Drug Smuggling and the Stability of Fragile State: The Diverging Trajectories of Mali and Niger'. *Journal of Intervention and Statebuilding* (2021): 3

Reich, Robert. *Beyond Outrage: Expanded Edition: What has Gone Wrong with Our Economy and Our Democracy, and How to Fix It*. New York: Vintage Books, 2012

Rieff, David. 'The False Dawn of Civil Society'. *The Nation*, 4 February 1999

Ruggie, John Gerard. 'Multinationals as global institution: Power, authority and relative autonomy'. *Regulation & Governance* 12 (2018): 317–33

Sasse, Tom, et al. *Government Outsourcing: When and How to Bring Public Services Back Into Government Hands*. London: Institute for Government, 2020

Scruton, Roger. *Conservatism*. London: Profile Books, 2017

Seligman, Adam. *The Idea of Civil Society*. Princeton: Princeton University Press, 1995

BIBLIOGRAPHY

Skinner, Quentin. 'The State'. In *Contemporary Political Philosophy: An Anthology*, ed. Philip Pettit and Robert Goodin. Oxford: Blackwell, 1997

Sørensen, Georg. *The Transformation of the State: Beyond the Myth of Retreat.* Basingstoke: Palgrave Macmillan, 2004

Stedman Jones, Daniel. Masters of the Universe: *Hayek, Friedman, and the Birth of Neoliberal Politics*. Princeton and Oxford: Princeton University Press, 2012

Steger, Manfred, and Ravi Roy. *Neoliberalism: A Very Short Introduction*. Oxford: Oxford University Press, 2020

Stiglitz, Joseph. *Globalization and Its Discontents*. London and New York: Allen Lane, 2002

Strange, Susan. *The Retreat of the State: The Diffusion of Power in the World Economy*. Cambridge: Cambridge University Press, 1996

Streeck, Wolfgang. 'How Will Capitalism End?'. *New Left Review* 87 (2014): 35–64

Tepper, Jonathan. *The Myth of Capitalism: Monopolies and the Death of Capitalism*. Hoboken: Wiley, 2019

Tocqueville, Alexis de. *Democracy in America*, ed. R. Heffner. New York: Mentor Books, 1956

Van Creveld, Martin. *The Rise and Decline of the State*. Cambridge: Cambridge University Press, 1999

—. 'The Fate of the State Revisited'. *Global Crime* 7, no. 3–4 (2006): 329–50

Varoufakis, Yanis, Joseph Halevi and Nicholas Theocarakis. *Modern Political Economics: Making Sense of the Post-2008 World*. London and New York: Routledge, 2011

Verkuil, Paul. *Outsourcing Sovereignty: Why Privatization of Government Functions Threatens Democracy and What We Can Do About It*. Cambridge: Cambridge University Press, 2007

Vincent, Andrew. *Theories of the State*. Oxford: Basil Blackwell, 1987

Von Lampe, Klaus. *Organized Crime: Analyzing Illegal Activities, Criminal Structures, and Extra-Legal Governance*. London: Sage, 2016

Wainwright, Tom. *Narconomics: How to Run a Drug Cartel*. New York: Public Affairs, 2016

Wang, Shaoguang. 'Money and Autonomy: Patterns of Civil Society Finance and Their Implications'. *Studies in Comparative International Development* 40, no. 4 (2006): 3–29

Williams, Bernard. *In the Beginning Was the Deed: Realism and Moralism in Political Argument*. Princeton and Oxford: Princeton University Press, 2005

INDEX

INDEX

214

INDEX

INDEX

INDEX

INDEX

INDEX